# BEING A
LEASEHOLDER

BEING A LEASEHOLDER

The essential guide
to owning a flat

Nicolas Shulman

A News on the Block book

Published by
Adrenaline Media Plc
One Great Cumberland Place
London W1H 7AL
T: 08700 600 663
F: 08700 600 664
E: nic@newsontheblock.com
Web: www.newsontheblock.com

NOTE: Material contained in this book is set out in good faith for general information only and is not intended to be relied upon by individual readers in making or refraining from making any specific decision, whether commercial, investment or otherwise. Appropriate independent advice should be obtained before making any such decisions. No liability can be accepted for any loss or expense suffered by anyone as a result of relying in particular circumstances on statements made in the book. The laws and regulations are complex and liable to change, and readers should check the current position with the relevant authorities before making personal arrangements.

CONTENTS

···: **PREFACE**

This book is about flats. It is aimed at both current and prospective leaseholders and will prove an essential resource in understanding the rights, obligations and complexities of owning a flat.

The content in this book is equally relevant irrespective of whether you live in a house converted into flats, a mansion block or a new purpose-built block of apartments. For ease of use throughout, I have simply referred to the "block" or the "conversion" as the "building". This is the most neutral umbrella term available to encompass the various types of property that leaseholders own.

The management of a block of flats is complex and usually requires highly skilled professionals. This is because there are common parts, shared between all residents, that need to be managed and paid for. There are also special legal issues concerning leases, landlord and tenant matters, as well as a whole host of legislation that specifically affects flats – for example, the Commonhold and Leasehold Reform Act 2002.

The complexion of the housing market has changed dramatically over the past few years. There are several reasons for this, such as the desire for central urban living, government limitations on homebuilders' activity and an economic environment that fuels investor appetite for buying flats. Although the last official government count suggests there are 1.5 million leasehold apartments in the UK, this is now probably a vast underestimate. In the past few years, all across the country the building of flats has overtaken the construction of detached homes. More than 40 per cent of all private new housing registrations with NHBC are now flats – with detached houses making up only about a quarter, according to the Homebuilders Federation.

The growth in the flat sector generates a host of issues of importance to residents and all those working in the industry, such as managing agents and resident management companies. As such, this book will become of increasing importance. With more leasehold properties forming part of the housing stock, understanding the particular issues that leasehold properties present will be of increasing importance.

This book is not intended to be a legal tome, and consequently, detailed legal references to cases and statutes have been deliberately omitted for reasons of clarity. It should go without saying that this book is not and cannot be a substitute for professional advice. I am grateful to Geraldine Shorthall MIRPM of the Association of Residential Managing Agents, Justin Bates of Arden Chambers, and Nicholas Kissen and Peter Haler of the Leasehold Advisory Service for their comments in the preparation of this book although, of course, all errors are my responsibility. I must also thank Ben Lane, Jamie Reid and Mick Wright, who helped in the preparation of this book. I hope that between these covers you find an accessible and enjoyable introduction to the world of flats.

Nicolas Shulman
London, 2007

···❖ **FOREWORD**

I welcome this addition to the very slim library of reference books for leaseholders. There is a huge volume of textbooks on leasehold law and practice for solicitors, surveyors and other professionals but very little of use to the end user, the flat-owner.

Leasehold is a decidedly odd system, unique to England and Wales as the only mortgeagable interest in a flat, and one little understood by flat-owners. It is a structure that places the majority of the equity, the value, with the leaseholder but all the power of decision and budget with the landlord. In attempts over the past 40 years to redress these inequalities, the government has created a great scaffold of legislation to preserve the innocent leaseholder from the rapacious landlord. While the intentions are admirable, the overall effect is to complicate considerably the management of flats and to place large administrative burdens upon landlords and managing agents. In cases of leaseholder-owned freeholds, operating through a resident management company, the matter is further observed in that the innocent leaseholders are also the rapacious landlords and are obliged to observe all the legislative requirements to protect themselves from themselves.

Government has steadfastly resisted pressures to formally regulate the residential management industry, instead creating a secondary network of rules and regulations, in which a block of flats becomes a regulatable workplace the minute a workman enters the building, with statutory liabilities placed upon the manager, then reverts to a block of flats when he leaves.

All of this law creates an environment through which the leaseholder needs a guide, something provided by this book. It provides simple directions through a hostile landscape and should prove useful to both flat-owners and managers.

Peter Haler MBE
Former chief executive of LEASE

INTRODUCTION

Before any explanation or understanding of flats can be attempted, it is important to understand the ways in which property can be owned in England and Wales. You may have heard terms such as "freehold" or "leasehold" mentioned, without appreciating their significance. This chapter outlines the fundamentals upon which being a leaseholder is based.

Different types of tenure

Property in England and Wales can be owned in one of three ways: freehold, leasehold or commonhold. The method by which property is owned is called a "tenure". This term reveals the feudal origins of the English system of property ownership that survives to this day.

Freehold

In simple terms, freehold property ownership means that the "freeholder" has absolute ownership of the property. The freeholder owns the property outright forever: there is no time limit placed on the ownership of the property. A freehold property can be considered the ultimate form of property ownership, and a freehold is a valuable asset that can be bought and sold, inherited and mortgaged. Subject to statutory restrictions or common law rules, the freeholder can use and enjoy his property as he pleases. A freehold is sometimes referred to as a "fee simple" title or "fee simple absolute".

Leasehold

Leasehold property ownership means that the leaseholder has a right to use and enjoy the property for a definite period of time. The terms by which the leaseholder may use the property are governed by a legal contract called a lease. Flats are most commonly owned on a leasehold basis. Greater explanation of leasehold property can be found in Chapter 2.

Commonhold

Commonhold is a new form of tenure introduced by the Commonhold and Leasehold Reform Act 2002 and became law in 2004. The Act, which introduced the first new form of tenure since 1925, was intended to create a real alternative to long leasehold property ownership. In simple terms, commonhold allows for the freehold ownership of individual units within a block and the common ownership of the shared parts of the block. In a commonhold block, each flat (or unit) is owned freehold and the common parts (for example, stairs, lifts, corridors) are owned and managed by a commonhold association. The commonhold association is a limited company in which each unit holder has one share. Despite its apparent attractiveness, at the time of writing, commonhold has yet to make a significant impact either in property law or on the housing market.

Types of flats

There are various terms used to describe residential leasehold property, and it is perhaps worth identifying these and explaining the subtle differences between them.

Flat: This is the most common term used to describe single-storey living in the UK. Flats in buildings that were formerly large houses and have been reconfigured into individual living units are known as "conversions".

Mansion flat: This term commonly refers to flats in mansion buildings built in the early part of the 20th century.

Apartment: This term, borrowed from the American vernacular, has grown in popularity to describe flats in the UK. The word is usually associated with properties in new, purpose-built blocks, and recently words such as "luxury", "luxury executive" or "prestige" have been used to prefix the term in marketing brochures.

Penthouse apartment: This refers to the unit on the top floor of the building.

Duplex: In contrast to single-storey living, some units within a block are split over two different floors connected by an internal staircase. These are known as duplex flats/apartments or maisonettes

It is important to stress that, from a legal point of view, it does not matter what type of property you live in. If you are a leaseholder, then the law applies to all equally.

The flat sector

Because more flats are being built, there are now more leaseholders than ever before and therefore a greater need for people to understand the complexities of owning residential leasehold property.

As this book shows, there are many issues particular to leasehold property, as well as several complementary and competing interests within a block of flats. Apart from the leaseholders and tenants who actually live in the block, there is a vast community of professionals with vested commercial interests in the apartment industry, including: freeholders, property managers, chartered surveyors, on-site staff (such as porters/caretakers), lawyers, insurance brokers, developers, estate and letting agents, building contractors, and architects. Often, the only "common factor" is the block itself, with each of these stakeholders having their distinct interests cemented together in this fast-growing industry. Ultimately, this is "the flat sector".

With so many people now living in apartments across the UK, and so many people working within the residential leasehold property industry, awareness of the important issues discussed in this book can only continue to grow.

Summary

- Freehold property is the ultimate form of property ownership, where the property is owned outright without any time limitation.

- Leasehold property ownership means that the leaseholder has a right to use and enjoy the property for a definite period of time.

- Commonhold allows for the freehold ownership of individual units within a block and the common ownership of the shared parts of the block.

- The growth in the apartment sector over the past few years means that awareness of the complexities of residential leasehold property is of continuing importance.

01 THE LEASE

The lease is the starting point for understanding the operation and complexities of leasehold property. Unfortunately, not all leases are well written or easy to understand. This chapter will explain the importance of a lease and help you understand the most common terms contained within it.

© www.newsontheblock.com

What is a lease?

A lease is a legal term used in property law to describe a particular type of property contract. In many respects, a lease is similar to any other type of contract: it is a written agreement between two or more parties recording the basis on which the bargain between those parties has been agreed. Although, in practice, leaseholders may feel that they did not have much bargaining power when agreeing the terms of their lease, in law, the lease is a written record between the two parties reflecting their agreed relationship.

Usually, the leaseholder will pay the freeholder a sum of money ("consideration") in return for the exclusive use of the property. This will be in addition to any other sums that the leaseholder may have to pay during the course of the lease. Such charges (of which service-charges – see Chapter 3 – are one example) will themselves be governed by the terms of the lease.

The usual parties to a lease are the lessee (the leaseholder) and the Lessor (commonly the "freeholder" or "landlord"). In some cases, tripartite leases include the management company too. These are commonly set up by the developer in new-build blocks of flats as a method of securing the management for as long as possible. If the lessees are dissatisfied with the management of the building, tripartite leases make it more difficult to change the management. Ultimately, this would be a lengthy and potentially costly process. Finally, there are some buildings where a separate lease has been granted to the managing agents of the common parts alone. Situations such as these can also cause difficulties for the leaseholders when faced with unsatisfactory management. The solution in such circumstances is for the lessees to exercise their collective right of enfranchisement and purchase the freehold. Recent guidance from the Leasehold Advisory Service (LEASE) advises purchasers of flats to investigate the parties to the lease in advance and to consider with care any purchase involving a tripartite lease or a building where the common parts have a separate lease.

In simple terms, a lease grants the leaseholder the right to enjoy the exclusive use of a property for a fixed period of time, and it is conditional upon the observance of certain express and implied terms contained within the lease itself. Leases come in different lengths commonly 99 years, 125 years or nowadays even 999 years (sometimes also referred to as "virtual freehold"). When the time prescribed by the lease expires, the ownership of the property reverts back to the freeholder (called "freehold reversion"). The freeholder is then at liberty to deal with the property as he pleases (which may include the grant of a new lease). The freeholder is sometimes referred to as having a "reversionary interest" in the property, meaning the freeholder's right to take possession of the property on expiry of the lease term. A reversionary interest is a valuable asset that can be traded.

If your lease is about to expire, do not panic! It is unlikely you will be automatically turfed out into the street. Rather, the law (which is primarily contained in Schedule 10 to the Local Government and Housing Act 1989) will usually provide you with an opportunity to remain in occupation as a tenant. More commonly, however, you will have the opportunity to negotiate the purchase of your freehold or negotiate an extension of your lease. Although the law will afford you some protection in these circumstances, it is a technical and specialised area and it is advisable to seek professional legal advice.

At this point, it is extremely important to highlight a common misconception often held by leaseholders: a lease does not provide the leaseholder with entire ownership of the property. If there is only one piece of information you remember from reading this book, then that should be it. All a leaseholder "owns' is the lease contract; the property is ultimately owned by the freeholder. Shocking as it may seem, a leaseholder only has the right to use the property that is the subject of the lease for the period of time prescribed in the lease. The length of the lease can be spotted when reading the lease by the words "to hold" which will be located nearby. Think of a lease as a form of "virtual ownership" of the property for a period defined by the lease length, accompanied by legal protection of the leaseholder's enjoyment of the use of the property during the lease term.

Leases are valuable assets. They can be bought and sold for significant sums of money. Despite the imperfections of the leasehold system, some leases are worth millions of pounds. When a lease is sold, it will need to be "assigned" to the new owner, and this procedure is discussed later in the chapter.

Common clauses in a lease

In addition to the information set out in relation to aspects of the service-charges, the lease contains other essential information for leaseholders and for those dealing with leaseholders. Although the structure, headings and clause wording of leases vary enormously, below is a non-exhaustive checklist of items to watch out for when either checking rights and responsibilities of a leaseholder or administering the management and service-charge costs.

Finding your way around a lease can be daunting, especially where the lease is old and contains an intimidating legal font from years past. Even so, not all leases are readable, let alone readily understandable. Following is a simple route map to help you navigate through the complexities of your lease. At the beginning of the document you will expect to find the date the lease was agreed (the "commencement date"), the parties and the preamble (which attempts to put the lease in some type of context). Towards the end of the document are the "schedules" which are a good place to look for useful information, such as service-charge information. In between these elements of the lease are the operative clauses that contain the juicy detail regarding your lease. The signpost to look for here usually says, "Now This Deed Witness" or "In Witness Whereof", and from here you should continue reading.

1. Prescribed lease clauses

This is a new requirement for all leases created on or after 19 June 2006. These leases are required to contain the following prescribed clauses at the beginning of the lease:

i.   Date of lease
ii.   Title number
iii.   Parties to the lease
iv.   Property description
v.   Prescribed statements
vi.   Term of lease
vii. Premium payable
viii. Prohibitions/restrictions on disposing of lease
ix.   Rights of acquisitions
x.   Restrictive covenants
xi.   Easements
xii. Rent charges
xiii. Standard form or restriction on the property
xiv. Declaration of trust

2. Parties to a lease

The parties to a lease will be contained on the cover page and also towards the beginning of the document itself. There can be various terms attributed to the parties mentioned within a lease and these are:

Freeholder: This is the ultimate owner of the property, and to whom ground rent (if applicable) is payable. The freeholder will also have the reversionary interest to the property.

Residents management company (RMC): If applicable, this is the legal entity set up to control the management of the block, embodied in the lease and in which all lessees must be members.

Head leaseholder: This is the first person to whom the leaseholder has granted a lease.

Under leaseholder: This is the first person to whom the head leaseholder has granted a lease.

Leaseholder (flat-owner): This is the last person to whom the lease has been granted.

The residents association of a block is not (usually) a party to the lease. However, it is a representative body of the leaseholders.

3. Structure of ownership

The definition of the parties to the lease, usually contained on the first page, will demonstrate the legal structure and additional documents that may be required. For example, the lease may list a freeholder, a head leaseholder and the flat-owner. These can be unfamiliar and confusing terms for those new to the leasehold system.

Where there is a head leaseholder, it is necessary to have a copy of the head lease in order to cross-reference it with the individual flat lease to define responsibilities and obligations properly. The lease will clarify whether there is a RMC in place. This can usually be obtained from the Land Registry. In some instances, the RMC will be in control of the management of the building. This should be defined in the lease. Note: a residents' association is a formation rather than a grant or party to the lease and therefore will not be shown in the document. A residents' association (which is an informal representative body of flat-owners and sometimes their tenants) is different from a RMC (which is a formal, legal person) even though the body of its membership may be similar or identical.

In a mixed residential and commercial block, the lease may show a freeholder, a head leaseholder on the entire block, an under leaseholder over the commercial element and a further under leaseholder over the residential element and ultimately a flat lease. All the documents referred to would be necessary in order to establish all the facts in relation to understanding the rights and responsibilities of the flat-owner.

In the case of bad drafting and conflicting descriptions of head leaseholder, under leaseholder or sub-leaseholder, the demised (i.e. defined) area will demonstrate the "chain of command".

4. Definition of the share of costs

There is usually an obligation set out in the lease for the flat-owner to make a contribution towards the maintenance of the communal areas of the building, while the freeholder pays absolutely nothing. The lease will set out the share the flat-owner will contribute to all communal items listed, and this may not necessarily be confined to one cost centre. In some leases the leaseholder contributes to the repair, maintenance and insurance of the entire structure of the block but not the internal repair, decoration, electricity, and entry phone. If the flat in question has, for example, a separate side entrance to a garden flat and therefore does not participate in all matters relating to the communal internal areas, the leaseholder may not be required to contribute to the maintenance costs of these areas. The lease would therefore show a separate percentage contribution for each cost centre. A leaseholder should check to ensure that the contribution he pays is in accordance with the lease and that he is only paying for those items he is contracted to pay. However, in older leases this may not be easy to decipher, and it is understandable if the flat-owner is unclear regarding the correct contribution.

5. Flat responsibility versus block responsibility

It is important to identify which party is responsible for the maintenance of which parts of the block. The answer will invariably be contained within the lease, which will also describe which parts of the property belong to the leaseholder and which to the freeholder or management company. There will normally be a map or diagram of some kind providing a further illustration, with the demised flat and relevant boundaries marked in red. The division of responsibilities between individual flats and the block as a whole is one of the most commonly misunderstood, misinterpreted or overlooked issues in a block of flats.

Let us take a common example concerning the windows in a building, the maintenance of which is often a highly contested and complicated issue. The lease is frequently unclear as to whether the windows, window frames and glass therein are demised solely to the flat, and are therefore the flat's responsibility entirely, or whether only the glass is demised to the flat (in which case, repair and replacement of the windows is the building's responsibility), and window cleaning a flat responsibility. Commonly and perplexingly, the frames of the window are found to be the responsibility of the building while the glass within that frame is the responsibility of the flat-owner. A wise leaseholder who needs to replace his windows will liaise with the property manager or responsible party when major works are being carried out. The building will normally be scaffolded at this point, and costs can be saved by prior agreement and coordination. If the windows are not shown as demised to the flat, it will usually be the responsibility of the building. This will be listed under lessor's covenants to deal with all aspects of the windows. Cleaning is commonly listed under the lessees' covenants. Most leases, even if the entire windows are the responsibility of the flat, will contain the provision that the painting of the exterior of the window frames/sills is to be carried out under the contract for external decorations that is, it is the building's responsibility. This, of course, is to ensure consistency of outward appearance and preventative maintenance.

6. Flat doors

The lease should rule on the treatment of the external appearances of flat doors. For example, some leases demise the flat doors to the flat but retain control over the outward appearance of the doors. In these cases, flat-owners are not allowed to individualise the colour or style of their front door. This prevents a mixed colour scheme of front doors in the common parts. Such a rainbow of colour at the entrance to each flat would be unsightly and may harm rental and sale volumes in the building.

7. TV aerials/satellite dishes

Virtually all leases contain a prohibition against individual aerials or dishes being erected on the building because they are unsightly. A potential purchaser (especially a buy-to-let investor) should check in advance whether the building has an existing communal aerial system. The lease may prohibit the erection of individual systems and also not contain any provision for the installation of a communal system as a recoverable cost. This may be bad news for the buy-to-let investor because the ability to watch satellite television can be a common tenant requirement. The absence of satellite television may make the flat less attractive to rent. If a dish/aerial is put up anyway, this will be a breach of the terms of the lease, for which the flat-owner is liable.

In 2008 (latest advice), analogue television will begin to be switched off throughout the UK. That means that unless you have the equipment to watch digital television, you will not be able to watch television at all. This is an important issue for blocks of flats. The landlord, RMC or managing agent needs to consider this and make the necessary provisions throughout the block so that residents are not faced with a blank screen. This will almost certainly require the communal television systems in most blocks to be upgraded or entirely replaced, and residents to have a "set-top box" receiver attached to their television. There are several specialist suppliers who can advise blocks about preparing for the digital switchover.

8. Flooring

With the recent increasing popularity of wooden flooring instead of carpeting, this issue has become something of a thorny one. The prohibition against wooden floors was originally intended to avoid noise nuisance in residential buildings. Indeed, most leases demand the installation of full carpeting throughout the flat, with the exception of the kitchen and the bathroom. If wooden flooring is installed contrary to the lease provisions, the flat-owner is then deemed to be in breach of lease covenant and can be forced to carpet as defined in the lease. Given the popularity and often-cited health reasons for wooden flooring, it is common to find this issue now taken to court or a leasehold valuation tribunal (LVT). On application to the effective landlord, a conditional consent for installing can often be obtained. This is usually subject to no noise nuisance being caused to the flat below or adjoining, the installation being required to be of a high standard and acoustically sound, and containing the usual clause for removal and reinstatement should any noise nuisance be verified.

9. Pets

It is always prudent for potential purchasers to confirm in advance whether the lease prohibits pets. Some leases contain a clause prohibiting pets outright. Leases that have a complete prohibition against pets of any sort are enforceable and no requirement is made for consideration of any pets (with the exception of guide dogs, as mentioned below). Other leases will stipulate that pets of a certain type can be allowed only through a formal licence, which will be rescinded if any nuisance is caused. Other leases will allow a freeholder to make "rules" for the block, and it may be that these rules prohibit animals. Some leases are silent on the subject, which means that there is no restriction on pets of any type. In this latter case, if there is nuisance of any sort, the responsible party will have to rely on other clauses in the lease concerning nuisance and disturbance to neighbours in remedying a problem.

If you have a problem with pets, or want a pet, you should contact the effective property manager of your block. You can do this directly without the need for a solicitor. Most leases will have a clause allowing pets by consent. There is usually a procedure in place to apply for a licence by submitting a photograph and description of the pet in question. The consent can be rescinded if nuisance is caused. The most popular pets are dogs or cats, and neither is a particularly good idea in a block of flats. It is not usually in the animal's best interests in any event and can frequently cause disputes and real problems with neighbours. Conditions for having a suitable-sized and well-behaved dog usually require the animal to be kept on a lead, prohibit use of the communal gardens for "walking the dog", and restrict noise nuisance from barking. In the case of disruptive dog barking, this should be reported to the environmental health officer who has the powers to deal with the issue. The Disability Discrimination Act 1995 makes it more difficult to exclude guide/assistance dogs.

10. Washing/clothes hanging in windows or balconies
Leases are designed to pre-empt problems caused by people living in close proximity. The perception is that the external appearance of a block is not enhanced by the sight of many windows and balconies displaying washing or clothes-hanging. Many leases contain a flat-owner's covenant to ensure that proper curtaining or blinds are in place.

Occupiers of flats who, for example, insist on having no curtains or blinds in place and display a huge array of washing or have the contents of their wardrobe on full display in the window may be in breach of the lease (assuming the relevant clause is present). This is usually a huge irritant to other residents of an otherwise attractive-looking block but is not an issue the local authority or the environmental health officer are usually disposed to deal with. In this particular instance, if an amicable approach and follow-up in writing does not work, there is usually no option but to endeavour to enforce the lease covenant. It must be remembered that permission by the effective landlord is required before solicitors can be instructed to issue a warning letter. It is relatively unusual these days to find this particular breach of lease covenant. Most sub let flats are already equipped with blinds and curtains, and most flat-owners are sufficiently concerned with the external appearance of the block they live in to care about its appearance. However, if there is a problem and initial approaches do not seem to achieve results, the matter should be reported to the managing agents, RMC directors and freeholder, and a warning letter issued to the leaseholder rather than a subtenant.

11. Loud music/noise

This emotive issue may well be covered by a clause in the lease prohibiting the playing of loud music or instruments or general noise between certain hours. Legislation more commonly covers this effectively, with the ultimate power and obligation to deal with the matter placed firmly on the environmental health officer's department. The subject of noise in blocks is dealt with in more detail in Chapter 5.

12. Common covenants

A covenant is a term of the lease that specifies how each party will behave in respect of the property. Important covenants are usually expressly identified in writing in the lease, though they may also be implied in the absence of a written record. The part of the lease document containing the covenants is signposted by the words: "The Lessee/Lessor Hereby Covenants...". One common covenant is that of "quiet enjoyment". This means that the lessee is entitled to enjoy the physical use of the property without interference from the landlord. For example, the landlord cannot cut off the utilities to the flat, such as the gas and electricity. Nowadays, this is often an express term. However, even if not expressly identified in the lease, it will invariably be an implied term. Note that quiet enjoyment is not a "noise nuisance issue", and the two should not be confused. Another common covenant is called "non-derogation from grant". This means the landlord must not do anything to disrupt the lessee's use of the property once the lease has been granted. In other words, the landlord must not take away the right of the flat-owner to an area that he can use under the terms of the lease. For example, if the flat-owner has a right of way that allows him access to a path in order to go to the dustbin, the landlord must not interfere with the access to this path.

13. Formalities and signatories

The law requires all leases to be made by deed, and this includes any express assignments of the lease. A deed is a formal legal document that must be signed, and those signatures must be witnessed. Sometimes a seal is attached in addition to or instead of the signatures. Since 1989, all leases must clearly state that they are made by way of deed. The formal part of the lease is prefaced by words such as: "In Witness Whereof the parties hereto have executed this deed the day and year first before written."

Service-charges

All blocks have communal areas that must be maintained. The lease usually seeks to ensure that each flat in a block pays a fair and reasonable contribution towards the upkeep of the communal areas or costs that they all share. A service-charge refers to the amount paid by each lessee in respect of their contribution towards the maintenance of the common areas or costs of the block and other relevant services that the landlord provides. The service-charge can also be used to pay the annual maintenance of the common areas of the block and to build up a "reserve" or "sinking" fund for long-term care of the block (for example, lift replacement, external decorations) if the lease provides for a sinking fund. Usually, service-charges are paid in advance, either annually, half-yearly or quarterly and are collected by the management company.

The full story of service-charges is contained in the lease and reinforced by legislation. The lease will set out what costs can be recovered as service-charges and what proportion the flat-owner will pay towards these. This subject of service-charges is covered in more detail in Chapter 3, but it is essential to understand that the first port of call is the lease, even if the leaseholder has no knowledge of legislation covering this issue.

Block insurance

The lease/s will always place the responsibility of obtaining insurance firmly on the freeholder. In the case of a RMC being a party to the lease, it may sometimes be the responsibility of the RMC to place the insurance albeit in the joint names of the freeholder and RMC. While the lease will usually state that the insurance is to be placed with a reputable insurer and that the premium is to be recoverable through the service-charges from each owner in their proportion, it will not usually insist on revaluation, a subject that is covered separately in this book (see Chapter 4).

Ground rent

As this chapter has explained, a lease is a contractual agreement permitting the lessee the right to live in the flat for a term of years. Because the flat is part of a block built on land owned by the freeholder, the lessee must often also pay what is called a "ground rent" to the freeholder. This is to compensate the freeholder for the use of the land by the block. It is important not to confuse ground rent with the service-charge, but both are contractual obligations that must be fulfilled by the leaseholder.

The amount of ground rent to be paid, the review date and method of review (fixed or formula), the period to be covered (yearly in advance, half-yearly or quarterly) will be set out in the lease. The words "yielding and paying" can usually be found near to this clause.

From 28 February 2005, a leaseholder must be provided as a requirement for recovery of sums due with a demand for ground rent accompanied by a prescribed form of notice. There is no time limit on the rectifying of this situation by the proper notice being served, but the leaseholder then has 30 days from receipt of the notice in which to pay. This legislation supersedes any clauses in the lease advising that ground rent is payable where the demand is not made in the prescribed form, any period of grace contained in the lease, and any interest to be levied under the terms of the lease the duration of the 30-day period.

Failure to pay ground rent in theory could lead to forfeiture of the lease and the landlord recovering the assets. In practice, this rarely happens.

The breach is capable of remedy, the courts are loath to take away someone's home and there are many checks and balances introduced through legislation to prevent abuse of the system. In addition, the Commonhold and Leasehold Reform Act 2002 has prevented forfeiture of the lease in the event that the amount of ground rent owed is £350 or less or that none of the total sum outstanding has been unpaid for more than three years. It is of course possible for the landlord to pursue the amount owed without involving forfeiture and as a debt-recovery issue.

Ultimately, a leaseholder has entered into a contract to pay ground rent. There is no good reason for withholding ground rent, and even cases of genuine hardship can be discussed with the landlord.

Problems with leases

Problems with leases are many and varied and can be summarised in one phrase: "the original drafting". So, if you believe your lease is imperfect, at the very least you can take some comfort in the fact that you are probably not alone. Some common problems with leases include:

- the percentage contributions do not add up to 100 per cent (with either a shortfall or an excess);

- the leases were originally set up to force the freeholder to fund all costs for a year and only recover retrospectively once the accounts have been completed following the year end;

- the lease is silent on many of the subjects listed above, for example windows, TV aerials, pets;

- the lease does not properly define the element of the structure that is the block responsibility versus the individual flats' responsibility and forces a practical agreement to be reached between the parties after negotiation. Let us take balconies as an example. In an ideal world,

the structure of the balcony and how it is fixed to the block should
be considered a block responsibility, whereas any appropriate and
non-structural covering (such as decking, tiling) should be the flat's
responsibility. Arriving at this compromise, however, is not easy;

– leases structured so that a flat-owner is contracted to contribute to a
cost from which they derive absolutely no benefit for example all flats
sharing in the internal physically common areas, where one flat, in
fact, is excluded from these and has its own front door. Essentially this
flat-owner is penalised by the contract they have taken on. Remedying
this in a fair and equitable manner would require all other flat-owners
to agree to take on a larger contribution than they are contracted to,
and not surprisingly, there is huge resistance to this from the other
flat-owners;

– the lease is silent on the subject of subletting or assignment. This
may sound ideal for investor interests but effectively gives no control
over the tenants moving into the block. Where the lease contains a
subletting/assignment clause, this is normally accompanied by a
requirement to submit references on a proposed subtenant and an
application for consent. In this way, the building can retain some
control over tenant quality. Equally, where an assignment only requires
a notice to be served within 28 days after the sale, the ownership of
the flat may not be identifiable for some time, and the requirement for
notice of transfer and notice of charge (mortgage) is often overlooked.

Subletting and assignment

As stated above, the lease must be checked for the conditions applicable
to either subletting or selling the flat. Often the consent of or a licence
from the landlord is required. Although these conditions must be
reasonable, it is worth noting that there are always costs associated with
complying with these requirements. Usually these include legal costs and
administration costs to the managing agents (whose management fees

do not include dealing with these variable aspects and fall outside the scope of duties covered under their management fees in the contract). Legal costs and administration costs may be challenged for their reasonableness on application to a leasehold valuation tribunal.

Altering your flat

The lease stipulations can vary widely regarding alterations to the flat. Some leases require formal consent from the freeholder, and these are normally provided by way of a licence through the managing agent. A licence is a formal legal document providing the leaseholder with permission to carry out the alteration. A fee is normally payable to the managing agent for the licence. All alterations in the flat are likely to require consent, whether they be structural, internal or external (such as the positioning of a flue on the outside wall). The consequences of non-compliance can range from structural damage caused to the block by removal of a load-bearing wall or defective work carried out, to the higher-than-usual costs involved in obtaining retrospective consent for alterations on selling the flat. A common problem today is leaseholders unknowingly and unwittingly garnering a small portion of the common areas to facilitate alterations enhancing their flat. Ultimately, this may prove extremely expensive for the flat-owner. The landlord is obliged to take legal action against the defaulting leaseholder and require reinstatement of the portion of common area involved.

Lease variation

Sometimes the terms of the lease will be outdated, ineffective at providing for efficient management or just plain incomprehensible. To rectify this situation, the lease can be varied to achieve a more sensible and practical basis for the management of the building. There are only two ways a lease can be varied: by agreement or by order of the leasehold valuation tribunal.

If all the parties concerned agree, then the lease can be varied at any time by the unanimous consent of all flat-owners. In practice, variation by unanimous agreement is rare.

Alternatively, the lease can be varied by order of the leasehold valuation tribunal under Sections 35–40 of the Landlord and Tenant Act 1987. An application for a lease variation can be made by the flat-owner, the freeholder or any other party to the lease. The main grounds on which such an application for lease variation can be made are where the lease fails to make satisfactory provision for a reasonable standard of accommodation in one or more of the following areas:

– the repair or maintenance of the flat, the building, any land or building that is let to the flat-owner under the lease, or any installations or services;

– the insurance of the building containing the flat or any land or building let to the flat-owner under the lease;

– the recovery of expenditure under the lease;

– the calculation of the service-charge payable under the lease.

Section 162 of the Commonhold and Leasehold Reform Act 2002 widened the list of recognised grounds from which an application for variation can be made. In assessing whether the lease is satisfactory with regard to the above, the LVT will consider factors including:

– the safety and security of the flats and its occupiers, as well as the common parts of the building;

– the condition of the common parts;

- how service-charges are calculated, including whether interest is payable on late service-charge payments.

Although an application for a lease variation can be made by just one party to the lease, the law also provides a mechanism for the variation of multiple leases. Section 37 of the Landlord and Tenant Act 1987 allows the original application to be made in respect of two or more leases where the aim of the lease variation cannot be satisfactorily achieved unless all the leases are varied to the same effect. Where eight or fewer leases are concerned, a minimum of all but one of the parties must consent to the proposed variation. Where nine or more leases are being considered, the application must not be opposed by more than 10 per cent of the parties, and at least 75 per cent of them must consent to it.

Alternatively, Section 36 provides that where a lease variation has been applied for, any other party to that lease can request that one or more leases in the building be varied in the same way. For example, if a flat-owner applied for a lease variation, the respondent/landlord could apply for all the leases in the building to be varied in the same way.

Finally, it is worth noting that should the LVT decide it is in order to instruct a variation to all the leases, it can also order compensation to be paid to anyone considered to be disadvantaged by this variation. If the disadvantage cannot be compensated for, then the LVT cannot order the variation. Because this book is not designed to delve into the smaller detail of the law, it should simply be noted that any party/parties considering applying for variation must as a prerequisite check their grounds before applying to an LVT.

Losing your lease (forfeiture)

Forfeiture is a legal mechanism that allows the landlord/freeholder to remove the leaseholder and reclaim possession of the flat if there has been a breach of a lease covenant (or "term" of the lease). The law provides for forfeiture as being ultimate recourse available to landlords/freeholders to enforce covenants (such as payment of service-charges, administration charges or ground rent). The law of forfeiture has recently been reviewed by the Law Commission, which has recommended reforms to make the procedure fairer, more transparent and less open to abuse.

However, as the law currently stands, if a landlord/freeholder wants to invoke the law of forfeiture, he must first demonstrate that there has been a breach of a lease covenant. This is achieved either because the leaseholder has admitted the breach or by order of an LVT or court (including, where applicable, a determination that the arrears in question are payable and reasonable). Also, if arrears of service-charges, administration charges or ground rent are concerned, the total amount outstanding must be in excess of £350 or have remained unpaid for more than three years. Where the LVT or court has found in favour of the landlord/freeholder, the leaseholder may appeal, and the forfeiture procedure may not be commenced until 14 days after the time period for the appeal has expired. The reason for this is to allow the leaseholder to remedy the breach or pay any outstanding arrears.

Forfeiture proceedings are commenced by the service of a Notice of Seeking Possession under Section 146 of the Law of Property Act 1925. The notice must specify the breach complained of, provide a fixed time limit for remedying the breach (if capable of remedy) and outline any compensation sought. The leaseholder is given a short period in which to apply for Relief from Forfeiture. If the breach has not been remedied on the expiration of the specified time, then the lease is considered forfeit and the landlord/freeholder can take possession of the flat (after first obtaining permission from the County Court). Once possession of the flat has been obtained, the landlord/freeholder may deal with the property as desired, including letting or selling it.

Forfeiture rarely happens these days because the court/LVT is reluctant to take away someone's home and breaches of lease covenant are capable of remedy. Sometimes, a mortgagor (such as a building society or bank) may remedy the breach because their interest in the property will also be lost if the landlord repossesses the flat. Nevertheless, forfeiture does still happen on occasion. In one instance, a resident management company composed of most but not all the lessees, owning the freehold, actually received the benefit of a flat worth some £250,000. The flat subsequently sold, substantially augmenting the funds held by the RMC!

Summary

- Read your lease. This dictum applies to freeholders, resident management companies, leaseholders, managing agents and would-be purchasers alike.

- Adhere to the lease covenants. Again, this applies to those living in leasehold and those administering leasehold management.

- A lease can be varied, if necessary.

- There are only two ways a lease can be varied: by agreement or by order of the leasehold valuation tribunal.

- Where there has been a breach of the terms of the lease, as a last resort the landlord or freeholder may forfeit the lease and take back possession of the flat. Before doing so, the alleged breach must be determined by agreement between the parties, the court or the leasehold valuation tribunal.

02 EXTENDING YOUR LEASE

There is an inherent unfairness in the leasehold system that is a relic of its historical origins. An investment in a flat can be the largest purchase ever made by a flat-owner. The flat-owner's home is their pride and joy. Yet, the lease granted with the flat expires by one year annually. As such, each year the lease becomes less valuable with the expiration of time. To remedy this, the flat-owner can make a request to the freeholder that the lease be extended. There will be a cost attached to the lease extension. Thus, the market for lease extensions provides a valuable income stream for freeholders. This chapter outlines the procedure a flat-owner can use for extending the lease.

It has long been recognised that a lease should not become a diminishing asset. In 1993 the Leasehold Reform Act granted the absolute right to a qualifying tenant to obtain the grant of a new lease for a term of 90 years to be added on to the unexpired term of the existing lease and with a peppercorn rent that is rent-free, rather than ground rent payable. The Commonhold and Leasehold Reform Act 2002 has introduced provisions designed to reinforce and simplify this procedure. There is always a cost implication for the flat-owner obtaining a lease extension.

It is advisable to seek professional advice before embarking upon a lease extension, particularly from an experienced valuer and a solicitor. The valuer will advise the flat-owner on the amount to be offered for the lease extension in the notice, as well as responding to the landlord's counter-notice and any subsequent negotiations (including representation at a leasehold valuation tribunal (LVT)). The solicitor will help with the drafting of the notice and responding to any requests for further information including the response to the counter notice. The solicitor will also help with the conveyance of the new lease to the flat-owner.

Not all flat-owners are eligible by right under the law for a lease extension. To qualify, the following conditions must be met by the flat-owner.

a. the flat-owner must have a long lease; and

b. must have owned the flat for at least the last two years; and

c. the landlord must not be a charitable housing trust providing the lease as part of the charity's functions; and

d. the leaseholder must not be a business or commercial tenant; and

e. the building must not be within a cathedral precinct, or on National Trust or Crown property (though Ministerial statements before Parliament suggest that the Crown will nevertheless comply with the principle of the law).

A long lease is defined as:

a. a lease of a term of years absolute in excess of 21 years when originally granted (irrespective of the present unexpired term);

b. a shorter lease that contains a clause providing a right of perpetual renewal;

c. a lease terminable on death or marriage or an unknown date;

d. one which a leaseholder has held over at the expiry of a long lease, and the landlord has not served a notice terminating the tenancy;

e. a shared-ownership lease where the leaseholder's share is 100 per cent.

Where a qualifying flat-owner dies before applying for a lease extension, the relevant personal representatives may exercise the right for a period of up to two years following the grant of probate or letters of administration.

Having established qualification for a lease extension, the flat-owner will next need to research and obtain:

– the identity, contact details and lease length of the "competent landlord",

– the identity, contact details and lease length of any intermediate or head leases;

– a copy of the flat-owner's own lease and the registered title to the property.

A "competent landlord" must have a lease of the property with an interest at least 90 years longer than the flat-owner's present lease, in order to grant the required extension. In most situations, the competent landlord will be the freeholder, but this is not always the case. This is why it is important to correctly identify the competent landlord before the process begins. It may not always be apparent who is the competent landlord, but the flat-owner can use various means to obtain this information. As a first port of call for registered property, it is advisable to inspect the register held at the

Land Registry and obtain relevant copies of the entry relating to the freehold. Although there is a small fee charged by the Land Registry, this will reveal the identity of the registered owner, including headleases and mortgages. However, if this search is unsuccessful, or in cases concerning unregistered property, there are two statutory mechanisms that can be used by the flat-owner to obtain the necessary information. The Landlord and Tenant Act 1985 gives flat-owners a right to obtain the name and address of their landlord. Failure to provide the information within 21 days is an offence. Alternatively, the flat-owner may serve a notice on the freeholder, landlord (if different) or any other person with an interest in the property, requiring details of that interest. A response is required within 28 days, and there is no liability for costs.

In rare cases, a competent landlord cannot be identified even after a reasonable search has been conducted. If this is because the landlord is a company in receivership or an individual in bankruptcy, then the statutory notice can be served on the receiver or trustee in bankruptcy. The lease-extension process will then continue as set-out in the 1993 Act. However, if the landlord cannot be identified or located at all then the flat-owner should make an application to the County Court for a vesting order. The County Court, with reference to the LVT for determining the premium, has the power to grant a lease extension providing the flat-owner establishes eligibility.

More often, the competent landlord will be identified eventually. Once the competent landlord has been ascertained, the flat-owner is almost in a position to serve the statutory notice asking for a lease extension. Before doing so, the flat-owner should make the necessary provisions for funding the purchase of the lease extensions and any associated professional fees, such as those of solicitors and valuers who may become involved. Once the Notice has been served, the flat-owner is liable for the landlord's reasonable costs from the date the notice is received, even if the flat-owner subsequently withdraws the application for a lease extension. This can be a significant amount of money which is why it is prudent for the flat-owner to budget carefully in advance of triggering the process.

The process begins by the flat-owner serving a notice on the competent landlord. If the competent landlord is not the immediate landlord, then copies of the notice must be served on the other landlords and the competent landlord informed of to whom copies are provided. Section 42 (3) of the Leasehold Reform Act 1993 states the following information must be contained in the notice:

a. the full name of the flat-owner and the address of the flat;

b. sufficient particulars about the flat to identify the property relevant to the claim;

c. details of the flat-owner's lease, including the date on which the lease was entered into, the term for which it was granted and the date of the commencement of the term;

d. the premium the flat-owner proposes to pay for the new lease and any other amounts payable to intermediate lessees;

e. the terms that the flat-owner proposes should be contained in the new lease;

f. the name and address of the flat-owner's solicitor or representative (if one has been appointed);

g. the date by which the landlord must provide a counter-notice, which must be not less than two months from the date on which the notice is served

It is important to ensure that the notice is accurate and complete when served. An incomplete notice can be rejected as invalid and any mistakes or misdescriptions need to be corrected by application to the County Court. Understandably, this will incur additional expense which it is preferable to avoid. If the notice is defective, then the process may have to be recommenced. In these unfortunate circumstances, the flat-owner cannot serve the notice again for another 12 months. The avoidance of mishaps is one reason why it is advisable to instruct an experienced solicitor to draft the original notice.

The notice served by the flat-owner should also be registered at the Land Registry. In the case of registered land, this can be by a notice; in unregistered land it should by a Class C(iv) Land Charge. By doing this, the flat-owner gains additional protection should the freehold to the building be sold. This is because any purchase of the freehold subsequent to service and registration of the notice is made subject to the flat-owner's application for a new lease. The flat-owner's request for a lease extension must be dealt with as if the new freeholder had been served with the original notice.

Registering the notice is particularly useful if the flat-owner wants to sell the flat, because the benefit of the notice can be assigned with the lease. Therefore, the new flat-owner can continue with the procedure for the lease extension without having to satisfy the two-year-ownership requirement. This can be a major selling point, especially where the flat in question has a short lease (which makes it more difficult to obtain a mortgage and therefore restricts the potential pool of prospective purchasers).

Once the competent landlord has received the flat-owner's notice, a response must be provided in the form of a counter-notice within time limits set-out in the law. The landlord cannot ignore the request because service of the notice initiates a statutory procedure that the landlord is obliged to follow. On being served with the notice, the landlord:

– can request information within 21 days to verify evidence of the flat-owner's title to the property and period of ownership. (The flat-owner also has 21 days from receipt of the request to provide the information. Failure to do so would deem the flat-owner's notice as withdrawn, with the severe consequences described above);

- can inspect the flat for the purposes of a valuation (providing the flat-owner is given three days' notice in advance);

- must serve a counter-Notice on the flat-owner by the date specified in the notice

The landlord's counter-notice must contain one of the following options:

i an agreement with the flat-owner's right to and terms of the new lease (or a proposal for alternative terms);

ii a rejection of the flat-owner's right to a new lease, supported by reasons (which will need to be determined by the County Court);

iii in situations where the length of the lease is five years or under, a refusal to grant a lease extension by claiming a right of redevelopment (that is, an intention to demolish and redevelop the building);

Where option (i) is specified in the counter-notice, there is sometimes a dispute between the landlord and the flat-owner regarding the price of the lease extension or the terms of the lease. The law provides a negotiating period of two to six months. However, anytime after the initial two months have passed either party can apply to the leasehold valuation tribunal for an independent determination of the disputed issue(s). The LVT will not choose one party's valuation over another but will decide upon its own independent valuation.

If the landlord does not serve the counter-notice by the due date, then the flat-owner may apply to the county court within six months for a vesting order granting the lease extension on the terms proposed in the notice.

Once the lease extension has been agreed or ordered by the court, and paid for by the leaseholder, a new lease will be granted and conveyed to the flat-owner. Where there is an intermediate landlord (for example, where there is a headlease, sublease and then the leaseholder), the amount paid for the lease extension is divided between the superior landlords. The total amount paid by the leaseholder is the same as if there was only one superior landlord; it is the division of the sum payable that is affected.

The law requires the new lease to adhere to the following conditions:
- it must be at a peppercorn rent (no rent) for the whole term of the lease;
- except for some minor modifications (for example, to correct a defect in the lease) and certain statutory exclusions and additions, the new lease must be on the same terms as the existing lease;
- there must be a clause giving the landlord the right to repossess the flat for the purposes of redevelopment when the lease term expires. The right is subject to a court application and payment of full compensation to the flat-owner for the full value of the remaining 90 years. There are no mortgage implications connected with this clause;

Summary
- A lease is a diminishing asset that expires by one year annually.

- A qualifying tenant has an absolute right to obtain a lease extension for a term of 90 years in addition to the unexpired term of the existing lease.

- The process begins by the service of an initial notice by the flat-owner on the competent landlord, in which a price is offered for the lease extension.

- The landlord must respond in a counter notice, either accepting-rejecting the flat-owner's offer or stating that the lease extension does

03 COLLECTIVE ENFRANCHISEMENT

In simple terms, collective enfranchisement is the absolute right of 50 per cent or more leaseholders in a building to buy the freehold of the building. This was first introduced by the Leasehold Reform, Housing and Urban Development Act 1993 and was reinforced/enhanced by CLARA 2002. Collective enfranchisement (which is also known as Leasehold Enfranchisement) gives the flat-owners in a building total control over the property that they own.

There are good reasons to collectively enfranchise, which is why it has become increasingly popular in recent times. When the flat-owners collectively own the freehold to the building, they gain the power of self-determination regarding the issues in their building. In practice, this means they can control who manages the building and at what price. Also, all the flat-owners who participated in the freehold purchase can be granted a lease extension, which will make their flat more valuable.

To successfully purchase the freehold of the building, a statutory procedure must be followed. This is explained in outline below.

Qualifying for the right of collective enfranchisement

In order for the right of collective enfranchisement to apply, both the building and the leaseholders must qualify for the right. For the building concerned to qualify:

- it must contain at least two flats;

- at least two thirds of the flats must be leasehold;

- it must not have more than 25 per cent of the internal floor area used for non-residential purposes; and

- it must not be a building within a cathedral precinct, or a National Trust or Crown property (although there have been Ministerial statements in Parliament suggesting that the Crown will comply with the legislation).

There are also two circumstances where, although there is no right of collective enfranchisement, there is a right to renew the lease. One such circumstance is where the freehold includes any track of an operational railway, including a bridge or tunnel or a retaining wall to a railway track. The other situation is where the building is a conversion of four flats or fewer, the same person owned the freehold before and after the conversion, and either he or an adult member of his family has lived there for the past 12 months.

Having established that the building qualifies, it is also necessary for 50 per cent or more of the qualifying leaseholders in the building to agree to participate in the purchase. The only exception is where there are only two flats in the building, in which case both leaseholders must participate. A qualifying leaseholder must own:

- a lease that, when granted, had an unexpired term of at least 21 years; or

- a lease with an unexpired term of less than 21 years but with a clause providing a right of perpetual renewal; or

- a lease terminable on death or marriage or an unknown date; or

- the continuation of a long lease under the Local Government Housing Act 1989 following the expiry of the original term; or

- a shared-ownership lease where the leaseholders' share is 100 per cent

However, even if a leaseholder satisfies one of the above conditions they still will not qualify if they:

- have a landlord who is a charitable housing trust and the flat is provided as part of the charity's functions; or

- own more than two flats in the building; or

- own a business or commercial lease.

Once the criteria for qualification have been established, the lessees will need to research the information required for the preparation of the initial notice and the response to the counter-notice. For example, lessees will need to know:

– the name and address of the freeholder(s);

– information about intervening or head leases (including contact details);

– full contact details for all leaseholders in the building and details about their leases;

– information about any flats in the control of the existing freeholder and let on periodic tenancies.

Some of this information will be available from the Land Registry. Otherwise, it can be requested directly from the freeholder. The Landlord and Tenant Act 1985 gives flat-owners a right to obtain the identity and contact details of their landlord. Failure to provide the information within 21 days is an offence. Also, Section 11 of the Leasehold Reform, Housing and Urban Development Act 1993 gives flat-owners the right to serve an information notice on the freeholder. This requires the freeholder to disclose information about his interest in the property within 28 days, as well as details of any other freeholders or intervening interests.

In rare cases, the freeholder cannot be identified even after a reasonable search has been conducted. If this is because the landlord is a company in receivership or an individual in bankruptcy then the statutory notice can be served on the receiver or trustee in bankruptcy. The enfranchisement process will then continue as set out in the 1993 Act. Alternatively, the freeholder (if a company) may have been struck off or ceased to trade for some reason and its assets passed to the Crown through the Treasury solicitor. In such circumstances, the Treasury solicitor will usually sell the freehold to the leaseholders at the open market value. There is no need or legal obligation to serve the initial notice on the Treasury solicitor. However, if the freeholder cannot be identified or located at all then the leaseholders should make an application to the County Court for a vesting order. The County Court, with reference to the leasehold valuation tribunal (LVT) for determining the premium, has the power to grant a lease extension providing the flat-owner establishes eligibility.

The participation agreement

Once it has been established that the building qualifies for collective enfranchisement and there are enough qualifying leaseholders within the building who agree to purchase the freehold, it is advisable to conclude a participation agreement. This is because the purchase of the freehold of a building is a cooperative undertaking between several people. Each participating leaseholder is dependent on the others to perform – especially with regard to their promised financial contributions for the purchase to stand a chance of success. It is not a good idea to proceed with collective enfranchisement if doing so depends on orally uttered promises alone. Therefore, if the participating leaseholders are bound together by a formal legal contract, this can provide a structure for ensuring contributions are collected and organising other parts of this complex procedure. Otherwise, any shortfall in contributions would have to be made up by those participating leaseholders who remain. Alternatively, if each participating leaseholder pays their full contribution up front, the need for a participation agreement may be avoided.

Since there is no legal requirement to have a participation agreement, there is no prescribed format for its contents. However, guidance from the Leasehold Advisory Service (LEASE) recommends the following key points should be included:

- an agreement between the participating leaseholders to formally instruct the nominee purchaser and proceed to serve the initial notice;
- an agreement that no participating leaseholder will withdraw from the process, thereby endangering the whole process and possibly requiring all the other participating leaseholders to pay more in covering the shortfall and any associated costs;

- a person who is in control of the process on behalf of all participating leaseholders should be identified and given authority to instruct solicitors and valuers as necessary as a single point of contact;

- each individual contribution (towards both the purchase cost and transaction/professional fees) should be specified;

- an agreement that there will be no delay in the provision of promised financial contributions, which again could endanger the process ;

- a statement that once the freehold has been purchased, each participating leaseholder will be granted a new lease;

Ideally, the participation agreement should be agreed at the inception of the enfranchisement process and, at the latest, before service of the initial notice. A solicitor can advise on the preparation of an appropriate participation agreement, although a template agreement (for guidance purposes only) has been included in the Appendix to this book. Each participating leaseholder should also seek legal advice about their own circumstances before agreeing to be bound by the proposed participation agreement.

The Commonhold and Leasehold Reform Act 2002 requires a formal invitation to participate to be served on all non-participating leaseholders. Although this provision has not yet become law, it is good practice to emulate this provision by asking all non-participating leaseholders to participate if they wish to do so.

The nominee purchaser

The nominee purchaser is the person named in the Initial notice who will acquire the freehold and become the new landlord of the building. Although the Commonhold and Leasehold Reform Act 2002 provided that the nominee purchaser would be a "Right to Enfranchise" (RTE) company, these provisions have not yet come into force.

The nominee purchaser can be a real or legal person (such as a company or a trust). Sometimes, a third-party company (for example, a housing association) will be asked by the leaseholders to become the nominee purchaser. However, in most cases, the leaseholders will form a company specifically for the purpose of acquiring the freehold to their building. Each participating flat-owner will own a share in the company. It is important to seek professional legal advice with regard to the formation of a company with the appropriate memorandum and articles of association in order to govern voting rights and control of shares.

Funding the purchase

Collective enfranchisement can be expensive, both in terms of the purchase price of the freehold and the associated transaction costs involved (such as professional fees of valuers and solicitors). Before serving the initial notice, the participating leaseholders should seek professional advice from a valuer regarding the estimated cost of enfranchising their building and establish a fund (including any loans and mortgages) to cover those costs. Once the initial notice has been served, the participating leaseholders will be liable to pay not only their own costs but those of the existing landlord too – even if they subsequently withdraw from the purchase. This is another reason why it is prudent for the flat-owners to finalise a participation agreement in advance of proceeding with the freehold purchase.

The initial notice

The collective-enfranchisement process commences by the service of a formal Initial notice on the existing landlord by the nominee purchaser. This triggers the moment by which all participating leaseholders are jointly and severally liable for their own costs and those of the landlord, as well as the valuation date (even if the negotiation/determination of the price takes longer).

Section 13(3) of the Leasehold Reform Act 1993 states that the following information must be contained in the initial notice (which must be signed by each participating leaseholder):

- a statement explaining that the building qualifies for the right of collective enfranchisement on the relevant date;

- particulars of the building and an accompanying plan (including any additional land the leaseholders want to acquire, such as garages, and any rights of way not to be acquired);

- information about any intermediate interests that will need to be acquired (such as an intervening head lease);

- the purchase price offered (including the price for any intervening interests);

- the full names and addresses of all the qualifying leaseholders and particulars about their leases;

- the name and address of the nominee purchaser;

- the date by which the counter-notice must be served by the landlord.

It is important to ensure that the Initial notice is accurate and complete when served. An incomplete Initial notice can be rejected as invalid, and any mistakes or misdescriptions need to be corrected by application to the County Court. Understandably, this will incur additional expense, which it is preferable to avoid. If the initial notice is defective, then it may have to be withdrawn or deemed to be withdrawn. In these unfortunate circumstances, the leaseholders cannot serve the initial notice again for another 12 months. The avoidance of mishaps is one reason why it is advisable to instruct an experienced solicitor to draft the original initial notice.

The initial notice should also be registered at the Land Registry. In the case of registered land, this can be as an "estate contract" or a unilateral notice under the Land Registration Act 2002. Where unregistered land is concerned, it should by a Class C(iv) Land Charge. By doing this, the nominee purchaser gains additional protection should the freehold to the building be sold. This is because any purchaser of the freehold subsequent to service and registration of the initial notice is made subject to application for enfranchisement. The nominee purchaser's request for collective enfranchisement must be dealt with as if the new freeholder had been served with the initial notice.

The counter-notice

Once the freeholder has received the initial notice, a response must be provided in the form of a counter-notice within time limits set out in the law. The freeholder cannot ignore the request because service of the initial notice initiates a statutory procedure that the landlord is obliged to follow. On being served with the initial notice, the freeholder:

– can request information within 21 days to verify evidence of the participating leaseholders' title to their flats. (The nominee purchaser also has 21 days from receipt of the request to provide the information.

Failure to do so would deem the initial notice as withdrawn, with the severe consequences described above.)

– can inspect the building and the participating leaseholders' flats for the purposes of a valuation (providing the flat-owner is given 10 days' notice in advance);

– must serve a counter-notice on the nominee purchaser by the date specified in the notice.

The freeholder's counter-notice must contain one of the following options:

i an agreement with the nominee purchaser's right to the freehold and terms of the purchase (or a proposal for alternative terms); or

ii a rejection of the nominee purchasers' right to the freehold, supported by reasons (which will need to be determined by the County Court); or

iii in situations where two thirds of all the leases in the building have a remaining term of five years or under, a statement that an application for a court order will be made preventing the exercise of the right of enfranchisement because the freeholder intends to redevelop the whole or a substantial part of the building.

Where option (i) is specified in the counter-notice, there is sometimes a dispute between the freeholder and the nominee purchaser regarding the price of the freehold or the terms of the purchase. The law provides a negotiating period of two to six months. However, anytime after the initial two months have passed, either party can apply to the LVT for an independent determination of the disputed issue(s).

If the freeholder does not serve the counter-notice by the due date, then the nominee purchaser may apply to the County Court within six months for a vesting order transferring the freehold on the terms proposed in the initial notice.

The right of first refusal

Finally, it is worth noting the right of first refusal. Part 1 of the Landlord and Tenant Act 1987 (as amended by the Housing Act 1996) compels a freeholder who intends to sell his interest in a building containing flats to offer the freehold to the flat-owners before it is offered elsewhere, such as on the open market. Depending on the proposed method of sale, the freeholder must serve a notice on the flat-owners in one of the prescribed formats set out in Section 5 of the above Act. The lessees must be given time to consider the offer, during which the freehold cannot be offered to anyone else. If the lessees decide to accept the offer, then they will successfully own the freehold to their building. By contrast, if they decide not to accept the offer, then the freeholder knows he can sell his interest, having properly offered the lessees of the building their right of first refusal.

Failure to provide the statutory notice of first refusal is a criminal offence punishable on conviction by a fine of up to £5,000. Moreover, the disenfranchised flat-owners can demand information on the sale and the price paid and force the new freeholder (and any subsequent freehold purchaser) to sell to them at that price.

Therefore, a prudent freehold investor should serve a notice on the flat-owners pursuant to Section 18 of the above Act in order to discover whether the right of first refusal applies to the building and has been offered to the flat-owners. Section 18 provides the freehold investor with a method of contacting the lessees of the building about the terms and price of his proposed purchase. If the right of first refusal does not apply or the flat-owners decide to waive the right, then the freehold investor can proceed with the purchase of the freehold, having gained some protection against being forced to relinquish the asset at some point in the future.

The right of first refusal is a particularly complex area, where professional assistance is advisable.

Summary

- Make sure you take professional advice from a solicitor and/ or professional valuer before embarking on the collective-enfranchisement process.

- Check the qualification criteria set out in the legislation to see if your building meets the necessary requirements and can purchase the freehold.

- All participating leaseholders should enter into a binding participation agreement once it has been decided to proceed with collective enfranchisement.

- The initial notice is an important document that initiates the collective-enfranchisement process on behalf of the participating lessees by making an offer for the freehold to the landlord. The initial notice should be drafted properly by a solicitor.

- The landlord's counter-notice may accept, reject or exclude the right of collective-enfranchisement. There may be some negotiation required regarding the price or the terms of purchase.

- The procedures, time limits and valuation requirements of the collective-enfranchisement procedure should be carefully checked.

- The right of first refusal requires a freeholder who intends to sell his interest in a building containing flats to offer the freehold to the flat-owners before it is offered elsewhere.

04 CALCULATING THE COST OF A LEASE EXTENSION OR FREEHOLD PURCHASE

In previous chapters, the procedure for obtaining a lease extension or freehold purchase has been explained. This chapter will examine in outline the cost of purchasing a lease extension or freehold. Valuation issues are of the most important and complex factors to consider in a lease extension or freehold purchase, and detailed consideration of the calculations involved are beyond the scope of this book. In either case, the methodology used for calculating the cost is similar and shall be considered under the umbrella of a single chapter. Calculating the cost is an imprecise art best left to specialists, which is why it is always important to obtain professional advice.

The principles of determining the value of the lease extension are prescribed by Schedule 13, Part II of the Leasehold Reform, Housing and Urban Development Act 1993. Similarly, valuing the cost of a freehold purchase is set out in Schedule 6, Part II of the Leasehold Reform, Housing and Urban Development Act (as amended by the Commonhold and Leasehold Reform Act 2002). The valuation principles in each case are broadly similar and are based on the sum of:

– the decrease in value of the landlord's interest in the flat;
– the landlord's share of the "marriage value";
– compensation for loss arising from the grant of the new lease/freehold,

And in the case of a freehold purchase:

– value of other interests - for example, Rent Act tenancies, commercial properties, garages.

Each of the above shall now be explained in outline below to illustrate the valuation principles involved. However, the detail of making a calculation is beyond the scope of this book.

The decrease in value of the landlord's interest
The landlord's interest is made up of the net present value of the following items of future income:

– **the ground rent income** (the income from ground rent for the remaining term of the lease);

– **The leasehold reversion** (the value of the flat when the term of the lease expires and the flat reverts to the landlord).

In other words, if the lease(s) is allowed to run its course then the landlord expects to receive the above items of income from his investment. By granting an extension to the lease or freehold purchase, the landlord is decreasing the amount he would otherwise receive over the remaining lifetime of the lease(s). The landlord is entitled to be compensated for relinquishing this benefit. However, the landlord is not simply allowed to receive the money he would otherwise receive earlier than expected. Instead, a "discount" is applied because the landlord receives his money sooner.

Marriage value

Once the lease extension has been granted or the freehold purchased, the value of the property will increase. In the case of a lease extension, this is because a flat with a long lease is worth more than the equivalent flat with a short lease. For a freehold purchase, the increase in value arises from the fusion of the freehold and leasehold interests in the building, allowing the lessees to grant themselves longer leases.

Marriage value essentially refers to this increase in value of the property following the purchase. The difference in value between the current value of the property and its value post-purchase is by law shared equally between the landlord and the flat-owner(s). An exception is made for leases that have an unexpired term of at least 80 years. In such cases, the marriage value is deemed to be nil. Also, in collective-enfranchisement situations, marriage value is only calculated in respect of the flats of the participating lessees. This is because the landlord will still retain an inherent value in the non-participating flats. Marriage value is calculated by a specialist valuer with local knowledge of flats.

Compensation for loss from the grant of the new lease

The compensation element of the valuation provides the landlord with a remedy against any loss suffered by granting the lease extension or freehold purchase. The landlord may not be able to claim an element of compensation in every situation, and it commonly arises where the landlord loses an opportunity for redevelopment of the building, reconverting a house of flats into a single-dwelling house, or loss of access to a neighbouring property.

Valuation of other interests

In some cases, there may be an intermediate interest between the lessee and the freeholder (such as a head lessee). The intermediate interest will also need to be compensated for the purchase and therefore forms part of the valuation. The amount paid by the flat-owner(s) will remain the same, but the sum will be divided between all the superior interests in the property. The amount of the division will be calculated in proportion to their relative interests in the property, and this should be completed by a specialist valuer.

Valuation strategy

A valuer specialising in lease extensions would calculate the cost of a lease extension based on the above principles, using a combination of complex formulae, market knowledge and experience. However, because valuation is part art and part science, there is sometimes disagreement between the parties as to the cost of the lease extension or freehold purchase. A leaseholder should always try to achieve a price for the lease extension that is less than the expected resulting increase in value of the price of the flat. If a negotiated settlement cannot be achieved, then it will be left to the leasehold valuation tribunal (LVT) to decide. The valuer will be able to negotiate on behalf of the leaseholder and provide expert evidence to the tribunal, if necessary. The valuation date is fixed as the same day the notice is served, however long the negotiation and determination of the price takes. Once a price has been agreed, the leaseholder can decide whether to proceed with the lease extension or not. Yet, irrespective of whether the lease extension is purchased once the statutory procedures are commenced by serving the initial notice, the leaseholder must pay the landlord's reasonable costs whatever the outcome. Therefore, the prudent leaseholder will always obtain specialist advice before serving the initial notice.

Summary

- Valuation in the case of a lease extension or freehold purchase is based on the sum of:

- the decrease in value of the landlord's interest in the flat;

- the landlord's share of the marriage value;

- compensation for loss arising from the grant of the new lease/ freehold,

And in the case of a freehold purchase:

- value of other interests - for example, Rent Act tenancies, commercial properties, garages.

- Beacause valuation is a complex and important area, advice from a specialist valuer should always be sought. Details of specialist valuers can be found through News on the Block or The Royal Institute of Chartered Surveyors (the details of each are in the Appendix to this book).

05 SERVICE-CHARGES

Probably the most frequent and contentious source of dispute for flat-owners is the service-charge. Depending on the building, this can range from £500 to well over £15,000 per annum or more. With such potentially large sums at stake, it is understandable that service-charges are subject to debate. The service-charge is often at the heart of the conflict and identity of interests in a residential building. Leaseholders desire the highest-quality maintenance at the lowest cost possible, and achieving this delicate balance is not always easy. In a freehold house, the owner can decide when and how his home is maintained. However, where communal living exists (as in a building containing flats), the maintenance of the common parts must be more organised and the costs shared equitably between all owners. Leaseholders can understandably feel aggrieved if they are not part of the landlord's decision on how to spend their money maintaining the building. This chapter will explain service-charges and place them in context from the leaseholder's perspective.

What is a service-charge?

A service-charge is defined in Section 18(1) of the Landlord and Tenant Act 1985 as:

- "an amount payable by a tenant of a dwelling as part off or in addition to the rent:

- which is payable, directly or indirectly, for services, repairs, maintenance, improvements or insurance or the landlord's costs of management; and

- the whole or part of which varies or may vary according to the relevant costs."

In essence, a service-charge is the cost shared among the leaseholders for managing, maintaining and running the building. The freeholder has a duty under the lease to provide certain services to the building and is entitled to make a charge for these. In order to be chargeable, the item or service must be included within the terms of the lease. Each leaseholder pays a sum of money (usually quarterly, biannually or annually) towards the service-charge fund. It is from this fund that the costs of maintaining and running the building are met. These costs will be identified in the lease and will usually include: building and other insurances, contracts, electricity, utilities, any water rates applicable, repairs and maintenance, any staff costs applicable, garden maintenance or maintenance contracts, entry systems, landscape gardening or as listed in the lease. If a proposed cost is not covered in the lease, then it is not a recoverable item under the service-charge fund. The service-charge should not to be confused with ground rent or the managing agent's fees (which are just a component part of the overall charge). The service-charge is an unfortunate and inappropriate misnomer (for example, "I get no service, so why should I pay my service-charge!"). It would be more aptly named shared costs.

For example, most leases oblige a freeholder to arrange for the cleaning of the common areas. Most leases go on to provide that the freeholder can recover the costs of this service from the leaseholders. This is a service-charge. However, if the lease did not (a) oblige the freeholder to arrange for the cleaning of the common areas or (b) give him the right to recover the costs of doing so, then any charges that the freeholder incurred in providing cleaning services would not be a service-charge.

How are service-charges apportioned?

There is no prescribed method for apportioning service-charges, but the sum demanded must be reasonable. Unreasonable service-charges may be challenged in the leasehold valuation tribunal (LVT) (see Chapter 12). Historically, various methods of apportionment were utilised, including

- rateable value;

- equal apportionment between the units;

- on a size basis (square footage as a proportion of the whole);

- on a size basis (number of bedrooms and possibly bathrooms);

- "fair and reasonable proportion" to be determined by a surveyor, the managing agent or some specified expert.

To understand the calculation of the service-charge in your block, first check the existing lease. It will usually stipulate a percentage for the individual flat towards a particular cost centre (some leases give percentages to the different cost centres, which may vary -for example, if some flats are excluded from a contribution towards the list because of basement/ground-floor location). The total percentages throughout the building should, of course, add up to 100 per cent in each cost centre. This is not necessarily always the case – bad drafting of the original lease can cause many future problems. If this is the case with your lease, you should consider varying the terms of the lease under the procedure set out on page 31.

In new leases, the most common practice is for a calculation based on the internal size of each flat as a proportion of the total internal size of all flats in the block. This, of course, seems fairly equitable and is also the most simplistic way. A developing trend shows a variation of this method whereby the costs of internal/external works, maintenance of the common parts, electricity and cleaning are divided based on internal unit size, but the costs of buildings insurance, managing-agent fees, and accountancy/audit fees are split equally between the units.

In the case of the older leases where the method of rateable value calculation was used, the calculation of the service-charge had to be translated into a percentage schedule when rateable values became extinct in the 1990s. The sum total of the values in question was calculated and costs allocated on a proportional basis per flat. On this basis, size is not particularly the issue, since old rateable values tended to be levied in accordance with rental value. For example, a flat on the ground floor was deemed to be less valuable, because of security reasons, than a similar-sized flat on the third floor. Therefore, this would result in a lower percentage of the service-charge being attributable to the ground-floor flat and a higher one to the similar sized-flat on a higher floor in the building.

Sometimes leaseholders believe they pay too high a percentage contribution compared to their neighbours. A variation of the lease is required to reduce their contribution and force other leaseholders to contribute more than is contained within the agreed percentage allocations. Lease variations are discussed in more detail in Chapter 12 of this book.

The law relating to service-charges

The law relating to service-charges is complex and unfortunately not contained within any single piece of legislation. Unfortunately, there is no single piece of legislation called "The Residential Service-charges Act", for instance. Instead, the law is scattered piecemeal among many Acts including: the Landlord and Tenant Acts 1985 and 1987 the Leasehold Reform, Housing and Urban Development Act 1993 the Housing Act 1996; and the Commonhold and Leasehold Reform Act 2002 (CLARA 2002).

Without going into detail that is beyond the scope of this book, all the legislation mentioned above is specifically designed to protect leaseholders' rights in relation to service-charges, particularly the reasonableness of the cost and when it should be paid. Leaseholders have the right to challenge both reasonableness and payability at a LVT. This includes circumstances where the service-charge in question has already been paid and a budget forecast for the forthcoming year. Mere payment of the service-charge will not be considered by the LVT as evidence of an agreement or admission by them that the service-charge is payable or reasonable. Also, a challenge to the service-charge is not confined to the current or previous year's service-charges but can cover many previous years. For example, if the LVT, and especially since its enhanced powers under CLARA 2002, determines that the cleaning or insurance-premium costs for the previous four years were not reasonable, then any monies already expended above the level set by LVT as being reasonable become unrecoverable from the lessee. If they have been paid, these sums should be credited back.

By law, payment of a service-charge must be demanded from the flat-owner in writing by way of a notice that includes an address for the landlord in England or Wales. In addition, a new Section 21B of the Landlord and Tenant Act 1985 (which became law in October 2007) requires all service-charge demands to be accompanied by a summary of the rights and obligations of the flat-owners in relation to service-charges. A flat-owner may withhold payment of a service-charge without further recourse if the demand is not accompanied by a summary of his rights and obligations.

Timing is important when making a service-charge demand. In many cases, the lease will stipulate that the service-charge must be demanded in advance of any works being undertaken. However, sometimes the work or service is completed in advance of any payment being demanded. In these circumstances, Section 20B of the Landlord and Tenant Act 1985 applies. Within 18 months of the cost being incurred, the flat-owner must receive a demand for payment or notification in writing that the cost had been incurred and that he will be required to contribute to them by payment of a service-charge. Otherwise, the flat-owner is not liable to pay for costs incurred more than 18 months previously.

Within six months of receiving the service-charge demand and the summary, the flat-owner has a right to inspect and receive copies of accounts, receipts or other documents relating to the service-charge (see Section 22 of the Landlord and Tenant Act 1985). To exercise the right, the flat-owner (or secretary of a recognised tenants' association) must make the request in writing to the landlord, who has 21 days from receipt to reply. The landlord may either provide facilities for inspecting the documents (for a period of two months) or provide copies of the information requested. Although the facilities must be provided free of charge, there is a provision allowing the landlord to make a reasonable charge for doing anything else in compliance with the flat-owner's request.

It is a criminal offence for a landlord (except a local authority) to fail to comply with a request either for the summary of rights or to inspect supporting documents without reasonable excuse. Prosecution may be brought by the local housing authority or the flat-owner. On conviction, a landlord may be liable for a fine of up to £2,500.

The reserve fund/sinking fund

Historically, the terminology of sinking fund was intended to indicate amounts of money saved up over a period of time to replace a defunct item, no longer fit for its purpose. The reserve fund was used to indicate sums of money saved up over a period of time to cater for emergency works or compliance with the fixing or maintenance obligations contained in the lease. This may include, for example, external or internal redecoration, lift replacement, structural repairs or the requirement for a complete new roof where repairing, maintenance and patching will no longer work. Common usage favours reserve fund as covering all these items, and sinking fund is becoming an archaic expression.

A critical point in understanding the reserve fund is to ensure that the lease allows for its collection. If the lease does not provide for a reserve fund, it cannot be collected. If the leaseholders wanted to establish such a fund, they need a separate agreement among themselves to that effect. If such an agreement is revoked at any time, then the agreement to collect a reserve fund will be unenforceable and it may not be collected.

The amount contributed to the reserve fund must be reasonable. The sum in question is either specified in the lease or determined by the landlord. If the lessees believe the charge to be unreasonable, then it may be challenged on application to the LVT in the same way as a service-charge.

There are good reasons for collecting a reserve fund. The theory underpinning a reserve fund is that all owners should contribute to major works irrespective of the length of time they own their flat or whether they are in ownership at the time works are carried out. Irrespective of their period of ownership, they will have benefited from the use of the common parts and will have contributed to the inevitable associated wear and tear on them. It is only fair that a contribution to the reserve fund is made to protect future generations of leaseholders owning flats in the building. Whether a leaseholder is lumbered with the cost of major works should not be analogous to a spin of the roulette wheel; should be divided equitably among all owners during the existence of the building. In this way, a well-managed reserve fund means that expensive, occasional bills can be avoided and ongoing maintenance of the block can be budgeted for satisfactorily.

Those who question why they should have to contribute to a reserve fund when they only intend to purchase a flat for a couple of years and then sell on should be aware of the potential difficulties when selling. The first questions asked in preliminary enquiries by the purchaser's solicitor will ascertain the existence of a reserve fund, the size of the fund in monetary terms, and whether it is sufficient to meet the obligations under the lease for the long-term repairing and redecorating duties. If the answers are negative on all counts, there is likely to be either a warning from the purchaser's solicitor to their client or a renegotiation on price to compensate for the lack of a reserve fund. In the United States of America, purchasers will not buy in a condominium unless there is a reserve fund in place and it is adequate for its purpose. Unless the lease provides otherwise, reserve fund contributions are not repayable when a flat is sold.

Reserve funds should ideally be held in a separate bank account (assuming there are enough funds accumulated), interest bearing to the credit of the reserve fund and absolutely not utilised for the purposes of propping up the day-to-day service-charge fund or, indeed, legal fees incurred by a resident management company (RMC) at LVT or action against a developer or landlord. Reserve funds should be suitably ring-fenced for their purpose, because they are vital to the ongoing good maintenance of a block and thereby protect the value of the flats.

Paying the service-charge and collecting arrears

The dates and periods of service-charge payments should be prescribed by the lease. Leases are notoriously inconsistent as to whether the service-charge is collected in advance or in arrears. However, payment intervals may range from one year (occasionally) to half-yearly (which often involves less administration) or quarterly (most common nowadays). By strict interpretation, the collection of service-charges by any other method or timing is in contravention of the lease. It has now become accepted that it is in everyone's interest to exercise a degree of flexibility regarding the collection of service-charges, save to say leaseholders are not obliged to pay for any sum not provided for in the lease. Nowadays, service-charges are usually accepted on the basis of standing orders, direct debits, post-dated cheques, monthly cheques, and even credit cards. This reduces cash-flow problems for the building. The collection of arrears is not an overnight success story, and due process of law takes its time.

Consider the case of a small block of five flats, where two of the largest flats were in the ownership of one serial non-paying offender who was adroit at playing the leaseholder system and the legal processes, with its checks and balances to protect lessees' interests. The building in question suffered serious cash-flow problems over a two-year period due to non-payment and legal due process. Three small flats and their percentage contribution could not cover the costs incurred over the period, given that the communal funds were missing a large chunk. In addition, the freehold was owned by an RMC which had to make special shareholders' collections to fund the legal costs in pursuing the arrears and also to ensure that the building was maintained. In panic, the unpaid voluntary directors of that particular RMC voiced their urgent desire to find an investor freeholder landlord to purchase the freehold and then enjoy dealing with the recalcitrant owner of the two flats in question. Non-payment can hit the cash flow of small blocks particularly hard. Just one non-payer in a block of five flats is equivalent to 20 per cent of the service-charge missing, or 20 non-paying flats in a block of 100 units.

There should be no misconception with regards how efficiently arrears can be collected. In striking a balance between the competing interests in a block, legislation introduced in 1985 was committed to protecting leaseholders against rogue landlords. Consequently, the law is neither quick nor easy in the pursuit of arrears. Understandably, those law-abiding leaseholders who pay their debts on time and without challenge invariably cannot understand why their non-paying neighbours appear to "get away with it" and be subsidised by the prompt payers for long periods of time.

In addition - and as a word of warning – not all legal costs incurred in the pursuit of arrears may be recoverable. This, of course, may be particularly hard on RMCs especially with multiple or repeat offenders. Occasionally, the lease may provide a mechanism for cost recovery. Further details regarding the recovery of costs as a result of LVT proceedings can be found in Chapter 12. However, when costs are irrecoverable, this may make the arrears collection a wholly unrewarding and unpleasant experience especially when leaseholders have to live in close proximity to the neighbour subject to the legal proceedings.

It is not unknown for the non-paying leaseholder to repeatedly offend year after year, thereby dragging the block through an expensive annual jamboree of arrears collection. RMC freehold owners should be aware in particular of the costs that may be recoverable under the lease as service-charge items. If the service-charge structure and collection in the lease is so inadequately drafted as to make the building unmanageable, consideration should be given to applying for a variation of the lease. Ultimately, leaseholders who willfully and persistently default in paying their service-charges may find themselves on the receiving end of an application for the forfeiture of the lease.

Administration charges

A service-charge should not be confused with an administration charge. Administration charges are defined in Schedule 11 of the Commonhold and Leasehold Reform Act 2002 as:

"an amount payable by a tenant as part of or in addition to rent, which is payable directly or indirectly:

- for or in connection with the grant of approvals under his lease, or applications for such approvals,

- for or in connection with the provision of information or documents by or on behalf of the landlord or a person who is party to his lease otherwise than as landlord or tenant,

- in respect of a failure by the tenant to make a payment by the due date to the landlord or a person who is party to his lease otherwise than as landlord or tenant, or

- in connection with a breach (or alleged breach) of a covenant or condition in his lease."

Essentially, administration charges refer to the amounts sometimes charged by the freeholder in association with providing certain consents (for example, to make alterations to the flat or provide information when the flat is being sold). The administration charge must be reasonable and the demand for payment accompanied by a summary of the leaseholder's rights and obligations in respect of administration charges. If the charge is unreasonable or the summary not included; then the charge will not be payable.

If a leaseholder wants to challenge the reasonableness of the charge, an application can be made to the LVT. However, it is important that the administration charge:

- is not agreed or admitted by the leaseholder in advance;

- has been or is to be referred to arbitration or a tribunal following arbitration;

- has already been determined by a court.

Any of these factors will preclude any potential LVT application. When considering a leaseholder's application, the LVT will first assess whether the administration charge is variable or fixed. A variable charge is one where the amount is not specified in the lease or a formula in the lease; a fixed charge is specified in the lease or by a formula in the lease. With variable charges, the LVT will simply determine the reasonableness of the charge. In the case of fixed charges, if the LVT finds that the charge or the formula for calculating the charge is unreasonable, it may make an order varying the terms of the lease to a reasonable sum or formula.

Service-charge budgeting

In a well-run building, it is prudent to prepare a service-charge budget to estimate expenditure for the year ahead. Where a professional managing agent is appointed, the budget should be prepared in conjunction with them. A service-charge budget will also be useful evidence as to whether the eventual service-charge demand is reasonable (see Section 19 Landlord and Tenant Act 1985).

A useful starting point for preparing the budget is to review the last known full year's expenditure, and to have a standard format for presenting the service-charge budget each year. Adjustments can be made for any exceptional items of expenditure that may not recur, or future items of expenditure that are expected to be incurred. Account must also be taken of any proposed increases in existing contracts. General repairs are usually the most unknown quantity from all the cost headings separately identified in the budget. It is always best not to be too conservative when budgeting, otherwise unexpectedly expensive sums may creep up in reality. If there are any significant items of expenditure proposed or if the budget prepared is lower/higher than normal, then this should be explained to all flat-owners. Care must be taken in particular with regard to new-build blocks. Usually, in such cases, the service-charge budget will be considered a warranty, and if misleading could result in criminal proceedings being taken. Ultimately, budgeting falls somewhere between an art and a science, and the more experience the person who is calculating the budget has of the building in question, the more accurate it is likely to be.

The consultation process for major works or long-term agreements

A landlord is required to consult with flat-owners before commencing any works (including improvements) to a building or any other premises that will cost any individual flat-owner more than £250. In addition, a landlord is also required to consult flat-owners before entering into an agreement for a period of more than 12 months with a wholly independent organisation or contractor, that will require a contribution from any individual leaseholder of more than £100 (including VAT) in any one year. Examples of such agreements are contained in Chapter 9 on Maintenance. There are some exceptions,

– an agreement entered into before 31 October 2003;

– a contract of employment;

– an agreement between a holding company and its subsidiary, or between subsidiaries of the same holding company;

– an agreement for less than five years that was agreed when the building was empty (usually a new development);

– an agreement granted dispensation from the leasehold valuation tribunal (such as emergency works).

Whether it is for works, improvements or long-term agreements, if just one flat-owner is affected, the consultation process must be followed. This consultation procedure is made law by Section 151 of the Commonhold and Leasehold Reform Act 2002 and Schedule 1-4 of the Service-charges (Consultation Requirements) (England) Regulations 2003. The consultation process is based on the old Section 20 of the Landlord and Tenant Act 1985, and it is still referred to as the "Section 20 consultation process". The statutory procedure must be followed by both private and public landlords, and RMCs. Failure to follow the statutory procedure and consult with flat-owners means that the landlord will not be able to collect service-charges in excess of £250 per leaseholder in respect of the works carried out and in excess of £100 in respect of contributions towards long-term agreements.

Under the procedure, all flat-owners must be notified before any qualifying works or long-term agreements are entered into. The notice must invite flat-owners to nominate their own contractors within 30 days to be considered for qualifying works or long-term agreements. Estimates from nominated contractor(s) must be obtained by the landlord. Where several contractors are nominated, the landlord must obtain the estimate from:

– the contractor who received the most nominations; or

– the contractors in first place who received an equal number of nominations; or

– where no contractor is more popular than any others, any nominated contractor receiving more than one nomination.

Once estimates are obtained, these must be circulated to all flat-owners, who have a further 30 days to provide any observations about the proposals. Any observations must be responded to by the landlord. When the final approved contract is agreed, all leaseholders must be notified by the landlord within 21 days, except where it is awarded to a nominated contractor or to the lowest tender. Allowing time for the whole consultation process to run its course, including responding to observations, will usually take three months or more.

Summary

- A service-charge is the cost shared among the leaseholders of maintaining and running the building.

- There is no prescribed method for calculating service-charges. To understand the calculation of the service-charge in your block, first check the existing lease.

- The law relating to service-charges is complex and unfortunately not contained with any single piece of legislation. Generally speaking, the law aims to protect leaseholders' rights in relation to service-charges, particularly the reasonableness of the cost and when it should be paid. Leaseholders have the right to challenge both reasonableness and payability at a LVT.

- The term "reserve fund" now commonly refers to a sum of money saved up over a period of time to cater for emergency works, compliance with the fixing or maintenance obligations contained in the lease, or to replace a defunct item, no longer fit for its purpose.

- If the lease does not allow for the collection of a reserve fund, then it cannot be collected. Where a reserve fund is collected, it should be held in a separate bank account to the service-charge.

- Do not confuse service-charges with administration charges, which represent a fee charged by the freeholder for providing certain consents.

- Preparing a service-charge budget to estimate expenditure for the year ahead is not only prudent but could be useful evidence towards the reasonableness of the eventual service-charge.

- A consultation process must be followed before starting any major works or entering into a long-term agreement; otherwise, the full cost of the works or the agreement may not be recoverable.

06 INSURANCE

Insurance is an extremely important issue for flat-owners. There are three key types of insurance every leaseholder should be aware of: buildings insurance, contents insurance and directors and officers insurance. This chapter provides an overview of these insurance obligations, as well as some other lesser-known insurance information for leaseholders.

Buildings insurance

Every building must have insurance. It is a lease requirement. Someone must bear the responsibility should the building burn down or some other major catastrophe occur, because the building will need to be completely rebuilt to the original configuration.

Buildings insurance should be based on the cost of rebuilding. These costs should, for example, include demolition costs, professional fees and accommodation requirements for the owner for the period of time during which the block is being completely rebuilt. That is the worst-case scenario. The most common feature is that building insurance covers the structure of the building where most of the claims are made (usually water damage or property fire). Note that it is the structure itself that is repaired and redecorated, or sometimes the damage to those flats that have suffered "resultant damage" from one of the insured perils.

Building insurance does not cover repair, maintenance or wear and tear. It will not normally pay, for example, for the section of pipe that is broken. That is a maintenance issue and must be dealt with separately, but it will pay for the resultant damage caused by an insured peril.

Any flat-owner has the right to:
− request a summary of the current insurance cover;

− inspect the policy document or evidence of receipt of premium;

− ask for copies of the policy documentation and payment of the premium to be posted to him.

Index-linked valuation

The insurance schedule will show the amount of the sum insured. This is the amount of money that covers the rebuilding and all the associated costs (discussed above). On renewing your insurance once a year, the sum insured has to be looked at. Normally, under most policies it is indexed linked annually. However, index linking may not always take account of a rising housing market, the cost of building materials, the cost of professional fees, the cost of demolition and so on. Resident management companies (RMC) have no VAT-recovery status, and this should be taken into account when considering the sum insured. Therefore, it is prudent to look at a revaluation of the cost of reinstatement. Ideally, a building valuation should be done every three years, but most buildings will not do it triannually. Five yearly, unless market conditions are exceptional, possibly with index linking, is more often the case. This valuation should be done by a professional, who will apply the standard cost of reinstatement to the different parts of the building and produce a formal valuation that will then be sent to the insurance company.

A word of caution is relevant here: it has been known for people to find themselves overinsured on valuation due to continued index linking over the years, having started from perhaps too high an amount in the first place. Normally, it should be accepted that the revaluation will probably cause a higher premium (and perhaps this is why most blocks prefer to revalue every five years rather than the recommended three years). Undervaluation can cause greater problems in the event of a claim.

The competent person required to carry out a proper valuation must be an independent party. This is nearly always a chartered surveyor. This is not a job to be carried out by managing agents, insurance brokers or associated property people.

The art of valuation is based on technicalities. For example, the cost attributable to reinstating an uninsured basement is a different cost to that of reinstating the first floor of flats or the car park. There are also costs associated with the higher number of floors in the building. This makes the valuation an extremely specialised procedure. To achieve the cheapest possible valuation, it is important to give the valuer a set of floor plans for the building. The valuer can then identify the measurements for the appropriate areas and apply the relevant building costs to different perils. If plans of the building do not exist, the valuer will be forced to undertake his own measurements of the areas required.

This will obviously cost more money. A valuation must be carried out by a "competent person". Normally, a chartered surveyor is both experienced and qualified to undertake this task.

Employers' liability

Where staff are employed, there must be an employers' liability insurance policy in place with cover for at least £5 million. This will cover the costs of compensation and legal fees for employees who are injured or made ill at work because of the fault of the employer. The certificate of employers' liability insurance must retained and displayed prominently in an area where it can be seen by staff and others. In fact, the certificate must now be held for a period of 40 years.

Most buildings insurance has employers' liability insurance included. If there is a resident porter or other staff, then the liability is a very minor cost compared to reinstatement cost. However, the responsibility for placing the buildings insurance always rests with the freeholder. The freeholder (or sometimes a local authority as freeholder) may consider that they have no obligation to place employers' liability as they are not the responsible party for employing the staff. In those circumstances, employers' liability (if staff are employed) must be taken out separately – for example, by the managing agent. The managing agent will seek to recuperate this sum from the lessees, and because it is not included within the building's insurance policy, it will be more expensive to insure this way.

Third-party liability

Third-party liability insurance is essential to protect any claims, for example, arising from or relating to visitors to the premises or contractors working on the premises. Again, this is attached to the buildings insurance and is not a particularly onerous extra cost given that it is often included with the insurance package. The standard amount covered today is usually £10 million and the costs for having this amount of cover are usually not disproportionate.

Staff accommodation/common parts

Insurance of the staff accommodation is sometimes overlooked. However, if there is a resident porter in place, then the insurance for this apartment and, more importantly, for the contents of the residential accommodation provided (which are usually in the ownership of the RMC or freeholder) must be taken into account when placing the insurance. For example, if the resident porter's flat suffers a leak caused by the flat above and all the carpets and decorations are destroyed, including the entire contents of a kitchen, it could be extremely expensive to replace. Therefore, insurance should be in place for the staff accommodation. The same applies to the common parts, which will have the sum assured assessed in the valuation. The contents of common parts, that is, carpets, decorations, possibly pictures - are in the ownership of the freeholder or responsible party and must be insured under this insurance.

Trace and access cover

Trace and access cover provides financial cover for investigating the cause of a major problem where it is not immediately obvious. This should be part of the insurance policy, and it is prudent to confirm it is included. If a floor or ceiling has to be excavated in order to find hidden pipes that cannot be seen by any other method to verify the cause of the leak, the trace and access cover will pay for the excavation, making-good and remedial work required afterwards (assuming that the cause of the problem is found to be an insured peril). If this cover is used frivolously and work is undertaken, for example, where it is quite obvious where the leaking pipe is located, and if the cause of the problem is not found to be an insured peril, the insurance company can and will, and are within their rights to, reject the claim.

One recent example occurred where the owner of a flat was advised that the cause of a leak was from his boiler, but this was not verified. In the meantime, the flat-owner replaced the boiler in its entirety and then attempted to make a claim under trace and access for the cost of a new boiler. The cause was found to be a pipe, obviously broken and leaking for many years, that could have been spotted and reported. The claim was rejected, and no mitigating circumstances were present.

Loss adjustor

The most important thing to remember about loss adjustors is that their role is to assess the validity of a claim. They are specifically appointed by the insurance company to protect their interests and maintain a firm grasp on the extent of the claim being made. They must ensure that:

– the claim is valid;

– the cause of the problem has been stopped; and

– the quotations received are reasonable.

In some cases, the insurers may insist on appointing their own contractors, especially where they have received quotations that appear to be excessive. In other cases, the loss adjustor's involvement may lead the insurers to conclude a claim as swiftly as possible in order to mitigate the damage involved in alternative accommodation, further damage, loss of rent claim and so on. Ultimately, the loss adjustors' recommendation to his client insurance company is cast in stone and effectively his verdict on the claim.

Loss adjustors are not usually appointed unless the potential claim appears to be reasonably large. Once a loss adjustor is appointed, he will decide issues such as:

– whether the claim is valid;

– whether the premises are habitable or not, or

- whether alternative accommodation should apply, or

- whether the insurer's own contractors should deal with the remedial work, or

- whether the items being claimed for actually fall under the building's insurance rather than contents insurance;

- whether a claim for loss of rent is valid;

At that stage, the managing agent is not involved and there is no other interference from third parties.

The function of loss assessors should not be confused with those of loss adjustors. The loss assessor is an insurance assessor appointed by the claimant to protect their interests and to ensure that the resultant settlement is fair to the claimant. In effect, the loss assessors role is the opposite of a loss adjustor. Loss assessors are often appointed on the basis of no win, no fee that is, they receive a share in any resulting success in making the claim. Loss Assessors are not often appointed by the company controlling the building to pursue a claim on behalf of one of the lessees. Obviously, the responsible person controlling the building has a vested interest in keeping the best track record possible. Otherwise, the insurance premium will escalate following a bad track record, affecting all who contribute to the premium.

Content insurance

While the buildings insurance covers redecoration of walls, ceilings and, in some cases, floor coverings (sometimes including carpets), it must be understood that cover for all other contents of the flat is the responsibility of the leaseholder.

While it is not a legal requirement for flat-owners to have contents insurance, it is advisable. The leaseholder often disregards the implications a major flood or fire can have on the flat, particularly in terms of replacing carpets and the basic infrastructure of white goods in kitchens. Often in cases of subletting no contents insurance is in place other than that which the subtenant may hold on their own property. In many instances, the subtenants assume that their landlord's - that is, the flat-owners' - insurance will cover everything they possess. Again, this is a popular misconception.

Tenant's insurance

If the flat is let to a tenant, then it is advisable to ensure that the tenant has contents insurance that includes cover for legal fees and third-party liability. This will provide a further layer of protection for the flat-owner if, for example, there is a leak damaging the flat below. The flat below will be relying on the flat above to have cover and may consider taking action against the culprit flat.

Lift insurance (engineering insurance)

This insurance is usually associated with lifts, but it also covers inspection of any communal plant - for example, boilers, air-conditioning, window-cleaning cradles and eye bolts. Most importantly, it is an insurance which provides for regular inspection by an independent engineer. The reports on the lifts from the independent engineer should be forwarded to the lift maintenance company (which is an entirely separate entity). Any reported faults under the lift engineer's report must be carried out by the lift maintenance company; any recommendations should probably be carried out, although these are not obligatory. These reports must not be left to gather dust they are for action and onward transmission to the relevant contractors dealing with maintenance of the plant in question.

Directors and officers' insurance (D&O insurance)

A director of a RMC has a duty to act in the best interests of the company. It is because of their fiduciary position as directors that they have unlimited personal liability and may be subject to legal proceedings, investigations and criminal prosecutions. Liability is shared among all the directors jointly and severally. This means that even if one director has done nothing wrong, he may be liable because of the acts or omissions of the other directors of the company. If catastrophe strikes, then the directors may be blamed, sued personally and face unlimited financial liability. Even if a director has sold his flat and resigned from his position, there is still the risk of a claim arising for acts done while a director. The directors will not be covered by the buildings insurance or the professional indemnity cover of the managing agents.

Therefore, as protection, it is advisable for the directors of the resident management company to obtain directors' and officers' liability insurance. This will cover legal costs for defending the directors against a claim and the cost of any settlement. In addition, the policy should include "run-off" cover, which will indemnify any directors for a number of years after resigning their position.

Making a claim

If damage has been suffered by a flat-owner and they have become aware that there is a problem, the first immediate action to be taken is to establish the cause of the problem and for this to be remedied. It is important to remember that the insurance company will not pay for the same remedial work twice over. If remedial work is carried out before the problem is resolved and the problem then reappears, this will not be funded for a second time.

Finding and stopping the cause of the problem can take various avenues of approach. The main cause of damage in flats is through leaks - commonly lack of sealant around baths and shower trays, a defective shower curtain or screen, or cracked waste pipes that are hidden under the bath and not seen by the flat-owner. Removing bath panels periodically to check for hidden trouble that contribute enormously to identifying problems before they develop. Leaking roofs and, at the other end of the building, draining problems are usually immediately identifiable. Similarly, damp appearing from an external source, if not the roof, is usually from blocked or defective topper-heads, cracked down-pipes, or overflow pipes that are allowing water to splash on to the structure of the building.

Once the cause of the problem is established, the remedy will not be part of an insurance claim. It will usually be a maintenance issue, and in the case of an overflow pipe, this will be an individual flat responsibility rather than that of the building. Quotes should now be obtained for the remedial work required. In the meantime, once the problem is identified or noticed, the potential claim should be reported in a timely fashion. Depending on the building in question, this will be reported to the resident caretaker, managing agent or RMC director responsible, or direct to the insurer's helpline or brokers. Check that the appropriate channel of communication is being used, and if in doubt, report the claim to various parties while awaiting confirmation of who the relevant party is.

If you have sublet your flat, you must be aware that regular inspections by you or your appointed representative are required. While it will usually be a clause in every subletting agreement that your subtenant reports any possible damage to you, in practice this does not always happen. An insurance company may reject a claim based on the fact that has not been reported in time nor mitigated in any way over a period of time. A landlord of a flat in that situation may have grounds for deducting monies from the subtenant's deposit due to their breach of contract and failure to notify their immediate landlord of a possible claim. In practice, this is not always very easy.

Having established and remedied the cause of the problem, reported all information to the insurance company via the correct channel of communication and obtained two quotations, the claimant is then reliant on obtaining the insurance company's formal confirmation to go ahead with remedial works and with the preferred contractor. The insurance company may have appointed a loss adjustor, who is then in charge of the claim handling, or may have referred the matter to their own approved contractors and issued instructions accordingly. Do not start work until confirmation is received.

It is always important to ensure, in the case of water-damage claims, that the damaged areas are fully dried out before remedial work or redecoration commences.

While the managing agent will deal with a claim or damage to the common parts of the building, it is usually the responsibility of the flat-owner to obtain a minimum of two competitive quotations from their own preferred contractors. They should also sign the insurance claim form, since other parties will not sign this on their behalf. It is also the responsibility of the flat-owner to arrange access for works to be carried out and to sign off the work as satisfactory. This will need to be submitted when the final invoice goes to the insurers for settlement. Settlement will not be made until the final invoice is submitted and satisfaction confirmed.

Although some years ago insurance companies were not inclined to pay much attention to track record, insurers now increasingly penalise heavily for a bad track record. Many building insurances in the past did not have any excess applicable under the insurance policy. Nowadays, these excesses are frequently either imposed by the insurance company (because of a bad track record) and/or utilised by the company placing the insurance to maintain the premium on renewal at a slightly lower level. The track record for a building is now a critical factor in determining how much the service-charge will be affected by the rising insurance premium on renewal. All lessees contribute towards that premium.

Directors of resident management companies are now more diligent in their requirements for the insurance-claim track record to be managed efficiently. They expect a policy to be in place to ensure that claims are limited to the necessary, and all reasonable steps are taken to mitigate the number and amount of claims. This can take the form of introducing rules, regulations and procedures in the building so that the culprit flat may be called upon to pay the excess in a claim under the buildings insurance, that small works are carried out via the service-charge by a "small jobs" maintenance man without making a claim, and that all efforts are encouraged by the insurers to pursue recovery against any contractors carrying out works that are defective. To avoid making further claims, all claims can be scrutinised as to whether they are frivolous or exaggerated.

It should be borne in mind that the insurance on the building is placed in the name of either the RMC or the freeholder or jointly in both names. However, whatever the case may be, in the eyes of the insurance company, the client is effectively the RMC, to whom all the lessees pay a proportion of the premium. Insurance companies are somewhat loath to take action against a serial offender, since the flat in question is a part of the client company. In turn, this involves a client company taking action against one of its members. Diligent claims-handling is therefore essential because reliance cannot be placed on the insurance company taking steps to prevent the frequency and seeming negligence of many of the claims submitted for example, filling a bath, allowing it to run and going away for the weekend!

Problems with claims

Some of the most frequent problems with insurance claims are as follows:

- If the property is undervalued, all claims made against the property can be proportionately down-valued.

- If the cause of the problem has not been rectified, the insurance company will not pay twice for the same remedial work.

- If a problem is allowed to continue over a period of time, the insurance company will undoubtedly reject the proposed claim through lack of mitigation in allowing the problem to continue.

- If the roof has been allowed to leak over a long period of time, the resultant damage to ceilings and walls in the flat below will undoubtedly be rejected by the insurance company and will then have to form a claim on the service-charge.

- Be aware that lack of maintenance over time is not a basis for a valid claim.

Premature remedial works

The claimant may have obtained two quotations, selected the lowest tender, proceeded with the works and submitted the final invoice to the insurers, only to discover that the insurers have not given the go-ahead. This may be because the insurers have deemed both quotations to be excessive and obtained quotations from their own approved firms directly. Insurers will not settle the claim submitted on any other basis than at a price they consider reasonable.

An example of this is where a lessee of a flat had installed wooden floors (before the time when wooden floors have become commonly accepted if acoustically sound, even if the lease prohibited). He did this at his own cost by replacing the carpet (which was a requirement under the lease). He then suffered a major flood. The wooden floors in question were enormously expensive but had been installed contrary to the lease and without the landlord's consent. The lessee then proceeded to have floors in two large rooms totally replaced with new wooden flooring while waiting for the loss adjustor's inspection. There followed a protracted disagreement lasting for some six months, and the insurance company finally settled for the sum of £1,500 in total, having also ascertained that the landlord's consent had not been given for the floors in question, and taking into account the ruined skirting boards. This settlement of £1,500 represented 9 per cent of the total cost to the lessee for all works carried out prior to any approval being given.

Be careful about postponing works. At a certain stage, the insurance company will close its file if they are not notified as to why the work has been delayed, when they will be carried out and when they can expect the final invoice. The claim will not be reopened if the claimant has allowed it to be delayed beyond a reasonable time.

The situation sometimes arises where the preferred contractor is suddenly engaged in works elsewhere and has advised that he cannot carry out the confirmed works within a reasonable timescale. In these circumstances, it is advisable to apply to the insurers to substitute another contractor but at the same price as they have previously approved.

Do not assume that the condition of the flat immediately qualifies it to be uninhabitable and that a sojourn at the nearest expensive hotel is necessitated. Only the loss adjustor can confirm that the flat is actually uninhabitable (however appalling the damage may seem visually) and the level of alternative accommodation that will be authorised. Unless both these conditions are authorised by the loss adjustor, no settlement will be made, or possibly only a minor contribution will be made by the insurers.

There is an example of a lessee who, without any authorisation, decided that the damp problem in her flat was such as to cause her to move into a nearby, expensive five-star hotel for six weeks while furniture was being rearranged and painting carried out. On submitting the final invoice for her six-week stay in the hotel, she was surprised and disappointed to receive an offer of just £250. The insurers considered they might have approved a greater sum for a reasonable hotel and an agreed period of time had they been approached and consented in the first place.

Leaseholders have a right to see insurance policies and/or D&O insurance.

Summary

- Every building must have buildings insurance and directors' and officers' insurance. As well as this, contents insurance for individual flats should be considered.

- Ensure your buildings insurance cover is adequate and revalued periodically. If the sum insured is inadequate for its purposes, any claim made on the buildings insurance can be down-valued proportionately.

- Ensure your revaluation is carried out by a competent person with professional indemnity cover of their own.

- Ensure your employer's liability certificate is prominently displayed.

- Ensure that staff accommodation and landlord's contents of common parts are adequately ensured.

- Ensure your policy covers trace and access.

- Ensure that you understand who the appropriate party is for placing the buildings insurance. In some cases it will be the freeholder; in some cases it will be the RMC; and in some cases the managing agents will be instructed to ensure that the relevant insurance is in place.

- The provision for giving responsibility to place insurance is usually contained within the lease, but don't forget all insurance premiums can be challenged as to reasonableness by a valuation tribunal.

- Make sure you have engineering insurance in place covering all items of plant and equipment.

- While not obligatory, it is extremely prudent for any flat-owner to maintain contents insurance cover that will also cover legal fees.

07 COMMON PROBLEMS

Inevitably, living in a densely populated residential structure has problems. This is a price paid for the benefits of living in a flat. This chapter will highlight some of the more common problems experienced by flat-owners in whatever type of building they may live, and includes some practical advice as to what to do about them.

Noise

Noise is possibly the most debated and most common cause of contention in flats. Noise has sometimes been known to cause internecine warfare between neighbours, and it remains one of the most misunderstood problems resulting from communal living.

For legal proceedings based on noise to have any realistic prospect of success, the noise must be shown to be persistent and regular. Ideally, it will have been diarised by the sufferer, preferably with witnesses and independent corroboration. Only armed with this evidence can the sufferer take any action. A common misconception is that all noise nuisance reported to managing agents or the head concierge will be dealt with immediately. This is not the case; a diary of events is required from the sufferer, no matter what the circumstances and what other party it is reported to.

There are three ways to take action against noise: through solicitors, the environmental health officer, or a private action.

It is important to note that since 1990 the environmental health officer at the local authority has been granted not only the most power to deal with noise issues but also the obligation to deal with noise problems. Dealing with noise in this way does not call upon the service-charge funds. If solicitors are appointed to take action against noise nuisance, there will be an immediate cost, because solicitors often charge on account for legal action to be taken. By contrast, a diarised notification to the environmental health department will result in punitive action being taken where the case is proved, at no cost to the leaseholders. Sanction includes fines of up to £5,000 and removal of the offending instruments, if it is a case of musical noise.

An alternative and often-overlooked option is for the sufferer of the noise to insist that the resident management company (RMC) or freeholder takes action through solicitors against the flat causing the noise. This may activate a clause in the lease that will demand an indemnity from the lessee asking for the covenant to be enforced, but this will depend in each individual case on the wording of the lease. This clause is usual in most leases, and the indemnity is against costs. The onus is also always on the leaseholder to bring this to the attention of the resident management company or freeholder. Many lessees are unaware of this provision when making demands for legal action to be taken instead of contacting the local environmental health department officer.

It is also possible for lessees to take out their own private action. This is under Section 82 of the 1990 Environmental Protection Act. If contemplating a private action, check with your local authority for their requirements. It should go without saying that bringing private proceedings against another leaseholder is potentially expensive, both in financial terms and when one has regard to the fact that, as leaseholders, both parties are likely to have to live as neighbours for quite some time to come.

Repairs

Repairing obligations to a building containing flats are contained within the lease and are recoverable costs under the lease.

Repairs must be carried out to the common parts. It may be tempting for a resident management company fresh from purchasing the freehold, to reduce the reserve-fund contributions for a honeymoon period while people recover from the cost of the enfranchisement. In this way, major works, external decoration and obligations under the lease are postponed for a period. Yet this is a false economy (external decorations are not cosmetic, but a function of preservation and repair). As matters deteriorate, necessary work can result in higher costs.

Repairs can be enforced if the freeholder, RMC or controlling party does not carry them out by applying to the court or the local authority for an order for specific performance. Also, a flat-owner can claim against the block for the cost of remedying damage suffered to their property resulting from neglect of the repairing obligations to the building.

One of the most significant causes of structural damage to a building results from water, in various forms. Problems with water ingress as a structural issue must always be addressed in timely fashion and never allowed to continue or the concern allowed to escalate.

Damp in individual flats is usually dealt with by an insurance claim for the resultant damage, providing it results from an insured peril and not from neglect or wear and tear. Disputes can arise as to whether rising damp is a flat problem or a building problem – assuming it is not due to lack of maintenance. Rising damp in a block is always a block problem and cannot be verified by obtaining quotations from contractors with a vested interest in carrying out works. Rising damp should be conclusively determined by a professional with no vested interest in the property or the repair work.

Dry rot and wet rot are often block problems, not individual flat problems. Any redecoration to individual flats resulting from these problems, however, is usually deemed to be the flat's responsibility once the rising damp, dry rot or wet rot has been eradicated.

Structural problems

Structural problems may be caused by the erosion of steel beams, the movement of porches or steps, or subsidence. The buildings insurance policy will usually carry an excess on any subsidence claim. If there is further subsidence allied to the same problem, it should be referred to the original claim, which will result in only one excess. Once suspected subsidence is reported to the insurance company, they will appoint an expert to investigate. Because the insurance policy will only cover one set of professional fees, it is advisable to report to the insurers in the first instance and allow their appointed experts to investigate, rather than commission a separate independent report for the building - unless of course the consensus of opinion is in favour of contesting the insurer's findings.

Subsidence is commonly caused by a lack of or inadequate foundations on shifting clay-based soil. This can be exacerbated by long, hot summers or the planting of trees in close proximity to the building. Lack of adequate control of these plants and trees (for example pruning, and containment of roots) can substantially exacerbate the incidences of subsidence. The insurers may want to enforce pruning and the containment of any offending plants or trees, where possible or necessary.

Pest control

Pests in blocks of flats are not limited to mice, rats and cockroaches. Due to a reduction in the regular collection of rubbish and more emphasis being placed on recycling, it is now quite common to have increased infestation. There are now many other pests causing problems in blocks. Fleas, mortar bees, squirrels, pigeons, foxes and even bed bugs have been reported. All pests in flats are a problem for the whole building and not just an issue for the flat where it may be perceived that the pest(s) originated. Pests do not restrict their activity to one area of the building. It is the responsibility of the whole building to deal with the problem and preferably, where appropriate, to have a preventative contract in place. Further details can be found by contacting the British Pest Control Association, whose details are in the Appendix to this book.

Parking

Where a building has on-site parking, it is second only to noise as an emotive issue. Problems fall into two usual areas: allocation and misuse. Parking is an issue that has led to serious arguments between neighbours and even resulted unnecessarily in vandalism, wanton damage and legal action between lessees. Some buildings have one allocated or demised parking space per unit. However, we now live in an age of two- and three-car families, and the original prescribed parking conditions contained in the leases are not always adequate. This situation is invariably followed by misuse - for example, the unauthorised use of parking spaces belonging to other lessees or visitors' parking (sometimes a planning condition). In some buildings, the available parking is either not allocated or demised and is insufficient in any event for even one car per flat.

The final sanction on private property is a clamping contract with a licensed firm. If all else fails, this is the final deterrent. Staff, unless they are licensed, are not empowered to carry out clamping. This should never be encouraged, since it will impinge on the ability of the staff to do their job vis a vis all residents in the block. Clamping contractors must be properly licensed by the Security Industry Authority (SIA) or they may be committing a criminal offence when clamping vehicles. It is also a criminal offence to employ or allow an unlicensed wheel clamper to operate on your land. More details about clampers can be found by contacting the SIA or British Parking Association. Whatever the legal or notional set-up with regard to parking for the building, rules should be in place for all to know and obey.

To clamp a vehicle legally, certain rules must be followed, such as:

- There must be clear signage in the parking vicinity notifying drivers that unauthorised vehicles will be clamped, as well as indicating the fee for releasing the vehicle and the contact details for the clamping agent.

- The fee charged for releasing the clamped vehicle must be reasonable.

- Once the fee has been paid, the clamp on the vehicle must be released without delay.

- Emergency-service vehicles, ambulances and vehicles displaying a valid disabled badge should not be clamped.

In some instances, clamping notices are displayed (for a small fee) but no clamping contract actually exists. This can lead to further exasperation, by flat-owners, tenants and lessees. Legal action requested by a lessee against a serial offender may require the indemnity under the lease (see under Noise, page 95-97) to be given by the complainant.

Anti-social behaviour

Local authorities produce much documentation on the subject of endeavouring to address anti-social behaviour for example, discussions with the landlords of a flat if the subtenant is causing the problem, discussion with parents if offspring are causing the problem, keeping full records of all persistent transgressions, reporting every incident to the freeholders or RMC, and so on. However, only the relevant authorities can apply for an ASBO (anti-social behaviour order). Private individuals who seek to control anti-social behaviour do so by seeking an injunction under the Prevention of Harassment Act 1997. Again, if the matter is referred to solicitors, the issue of costs arises. There is no easy answer other than to keep full records, report to the police every time an incident occurs and possibly refer the matter to solicitors with landlord consent if the problem becomes persistent and unbearable.

Rubbish

The indiscriminate dumping of rubbish by flat-owners and/or their tenants, the inability of certain residents to bag up their rubbish properly, the placing of dangerous objects in the rubbish (such as syringes and broken glass) and the habit of leaving leaking substances in bags (thereby damaging the common carpets) are contentious issues.

Properly behaved lessees and boards of directors often despair of ever teaching all residents how to deal with rubbish properly. This may become less of an issue now that the world at large and the government are becoming increasingly concerned with rubbish disposal. Significant funds are being invested and punitive action taken against irresponsible disposal. Some local authorities are now allowing co-mingled recycling, which makes it easier to deal with. Fines are being imposed on those who incorrectly bag their rubbish, leave lids open and place them in obstructive areas, or against people who do not place them in approved areas of the building.

The best advice is to make sure that the rubbish-collection policy for a building is formulated, known, displayed and regularly circulated. If a resident concierge or porter is in place, copies of the regulations should be available for distribution. The rules governing rubbish to be collected from outside the flat doors by a porter or a yard man and the times permitted should be notified to all, and rubber liquid-proof mats should be in place to collect spillage. Constantly organising special collection for non-domestic waste, such as cardboard boxes and mattresses, can impact enormously on a service-charge and will not get the popularity vote from the service-charge payers. Therefore, non-domestic rubbish collection should always be organised by the owner, not the service-charge fund. More information about rubbish collection and recycling can be found by contacting your local authority.

Mobile-phone masts

At the time of writing, there is no conclusive proof of any health problems caused by being in close proximity to mobile-phone masts. However, in blocks of high-rising flats in areas much prized by mobile-phone operators, the placement of mobile-phone masts is an extremely emotive issue. The freeholder has the right to install as many mobile masts on the roof of the building as planning permission will allow, and to collect the income from them. It is not surprising for the lessees in such a block to be united in fierce opposition.

However, assuming it is within the bounds of the lease, freeholders who place mobile masts on the top of blocks can often be prevailed upon to contribute some of the income to the service-charge funds. This will, of course, not always overcome all opposition. It is even more complicated where the freehold of the block is owned by all the lessees, or some of the lessees, in the block, and the RMC in question decides to opt for having mobile masts on the roof. There is an example of a prestigious block with a lessee-freehold owner that has three roof masts currently producing a substantial income each year. In this particular block, not all lessees are members of the freehold company. Although the majority of this income is spent for the good of the block, many lessees are in ongoing and extremely litigious dispute. The Mobile Operators Association has a useful website on this topic, the details of which are in the Appendix.

Smoking

By law, the common parts of buildings containing flats must be "smoke-free". This means that smoking is prohibited in these areas. Smoking within your own flat is permitted because it is exempt from the Smoke Free Regulations. Under the legislation, which is contained in the Smoke Free Regulations 2006 and 2007, buildings containing flats must be aware that:

- they must display statutory prescribed signage (the size and words of which are defined) in prominent positions notifying people that the common parts of the building are smoke-free. It is an offence not to do so.

- smoking in the common parts in breach of the Smoke Free Regulations is punishable by a fine of up to £200 on prosecution by the local authority.

- failure to prevent smoking in the common parts is also an offence. The landlord or RMC may be prosecuted by the local authority and fined up to £2,500.

- officers or rooms on-site in the building that are used by porterage, concierge or other members of staff concerned with the block must also be smoke-free and display the statutory signage.

More information can be found by visiting the government's website: www.smokefreeengland.co.uk

Summary

- For all the above common problems, always have a defined policy for the building. Have this displayed prominently, available to all on request, circulated periodically, spare copies on site, handed out by a resident concierge if one exists, and ensure that there is no excuse for all residents not to know the rules and regulations for your building.

- Always remember that transgressions have to be diarised by a sufferer, preferably should be witnessed and, even better, accompanied by independent verification.

- All damp and water-ingress issues must be addressed and in timely fashion.

- Do not allow any of the above common problems relating to the structure of the building to fester over a period of time. You endanger the properties, the integrity of the structure, the possibility of insurance claims and definitely the relationship between the leaseholders.

08 HEALTH & SAFETY

Whether you are a freeholder, right-to-manage company, resident management company, managing agent or self-managing, you should be aware of the following, which are intended as a basic checklist of health and safety requirements. On-site staff (including visiting contractors) will make the building a "place of work". This activates a host of legislation designed to ensure that the place of work is safe and that precautions, where necessary, are taken to minimise and reduce accidents. This list is not exhaustive, and in some cases there will not be a legal requirement to carry out certain actions. If the worst happens, blame will be apportioned by the Health and Safety Executive for failure to exercise a prudent duty of care. The advice must always be: if in doubt, check it out.

Asbestos management

Asbestos was widely used in the construction industry to insulate against fire and sound until the 1980s. Most blocks built before this time will have some amount of asbestos contained within them. The use of asbestos in construction decreased once it was discovered that it can cause several serious and unpleasant illnesses.

The Control of Asbestos at Work Regulations 2002 (which came into force in May 2004) place a legally binding requirement on landlords and agents to be aware of and to control any asbestos in the building. They must consult experts in asbestos management and follow recommendations made by them. There must also be an asbestos policy in place. This is usually done through an asbestos register.

The responsibility for carrying out the requisite survey/testing and maintenance of an asbestos register (or a record of the experts' opinion that no asbestos exists) is restricted to the common parts of the building. However, if the experts' opinion is that the potential for asbestos within the flats exists, this should be brought to the attention of the flat-owners for their own action. If asbestos is found in the common parts, the recommendations as to whether to remove the asbestos, contain the asbestos or label the asbestos should be followed. It is important to stress that it is not necessary to remove asbestos in all cases. In fact, to do so may be more dangerous than to contain it. Emphasis should be placed on the management and control of the asbestos upon advice from a professional asbestos licensed contractor, and flat-owners should not become over-anxious or panic about the presence of asbestos in their building. If asbestos is safely managed and contained it, does not present a health hazard. All contractors working in the building anywhere near the contaminated area should have the register brought to their attention. This should be done before work commences in any parts of the building. In the case of new buildings, it is always prudent to obtain a letter of confirmation from the developer that no asbestos materials were used in the construction. For further information about the control of asbestos, contact the Health and Safety Executive or the Asbestos Testing and Consulting Association, the details of which can be found in the Appendix.

Risk assessment

A fundamental cornerstone in health and safety is the use of a risk assessment to identify, manage and reduce health and safety problems. A risk assessment will:

- identify any possible hazards;

- evaluate the level of risk associated with the hazard (usually done on a scale of between one and five);

- ascertain what parties fall into the risk category; and

- plan to remove or reduce the risk(s) identified.

Risk assessments should be carried out by a "competent person" - that is, someone with the requisite qualifications/training, experience, licence (if necessary) and preferably professional indemnity insurance covering the activity. Once the risk assessor's report is received, it will be apparent which items must be attended to as a matter of necessity. Low-risk items can be noted and acted upon with less urgency. Usually, the managing agent will commission the risk assessment with the building client. Once the report is received, it is dangerous for all parties to ignore what is then on record, especially in the high-category risks. Ultimately, in the case of a serious accident, the Health and Safety Executive will review all records, actions taken and the degree to which a reasonable duty of care was exercised by all concerned - for example, client, managing agent, and contractor. It is good practice for a copy of the risk assessment to be held on site at the building as well as with the managing agent. Contrary to popular belief, there is no building that is too small to have a risk assessment carried out.

Risk assessments should be reviewed annually regardless of whether there are any directly employed personnel on site. Cleaners, gardeners and contractors will enter common areas from time to time, including plant rooms, cleaners' cupboards, garden sheds and lift-motor rooms. In the worst-case scenario, a record of annual reviewable risk assessment will go a long way towards proving that a reasonable duty of care was carried out.

Fire-risk assessment

The Fire Safety Risk Assessment Regulations came into force on 1 October 2006, placing a firm legal obligation on freeholders, resident management companies (RMC), right-to-manage companies (RTM Cos), landlords and managing agents to ensure that a fire-safety risk assessment is carried out. The consequences of ignoring this assessment are punitive in the extreme, culminating in enforcement notices, prohibition notices, unlimited fines, prosecution and imprisonment.

The purpose of a fire-risk assessment is to:
− identify any potential fire hazards such as sources of ignition (for example, heaters, lighting, electrical equipment);

− identify any items that can burn if ignited (for example, rubbish, furniture);

− identify who could be at risk in the event of a fire, especially children, the elderly, disabled or visitors to the building;

− remove and reduce the risk of fire (for example, by keeping fire hazards and items that can burn);

- protect premises and people from fire, should one occur (for example, by planning escape routes, ensuring necessary emergency signage is in place, testing safety equipment);

- record any fire hazards and action taken to reduce or remove them;

- plan how to prevent fire and how to keep people safe should one occur (you may need to coordinate with others in your building);

- where necessary provide on-site staff with the necessary training in what to do in case of fire;

- provide a regular opportunity for reviewing the fire-risk assessment, particularly if there are changes to the building over time in structure, personnel or residents.

The requirement for a fire-risk assessment extends to the common parts of every building containing flats, regardless of how small. In the case of a building becoming classified as a "house in multiple occupation" (see pp. 114-15), this requirement will extend into the flats themselves, seemingly with the same responsibilities being placed on all the above mentioned parties, as well as the flat-owner.

Electrical inspections

If any electrical equipment is supplied by the landlord, managing agent, or RMC, then it must be regularly tested and properly maintained. This is a legal obligation under the Electricity at Work Regulations 1989. Do not overlook the electrical appliances supplied to a resident caretaker/ concierge or cleaners. Testing and maintenance should only be completed by a competent person, and it is prudent to use an electrician who is a member of a recognised trade body such as the NICEIC, EEA or IEE (the details of which can be found in the Appendix to this book).

Water safety/*Legionella*

Legionella is a bacterium that can cause *Legionnaire's* disease by the inhalation of the bacterium through minuscule drops of water. It is not contagious. The control of *Legionella* is governed by the Control of Substances Hazardous to Health Regulations 2002 (COSHH) and general health and safety guidance. There is no need to have legionella checks carried out where the flats have no communal water tanks (that is, the incoming water supply is delivered directly to each flat and no storage is involved), there is no spa, Jacuzzi, communal showers, air-conditioning, cooling towers, ventilation plant, condensers, fountains or water features. If in any doubt, engage the services of an expert company to verify in writing that there are no areas that require checking and that could give rise to concern.

Where a water-safety check is necessary, the requirement is to control the risk of *Legionella,* particularly in any water-storage areas within the common parts. This includes a resident caretaker's flat or cleaner's cupboard. While leaseholders are responsible for risk control in their own individual flat, in the case of communal systems the block may be responsible. Ultimately, due diligence must be exercised to control the risk, and where necessary, lessees are to be notified that their own responsibilities include dealing with taps and showers within their own flats.

Working at heights

According to the Health and Safety Executive, falls from height are one of the single biggest causes of workplace deaths and one of the main causes of injury. As a result, in order to reduce death and injuries from falls, the government introduced the Work at Height Regulations 2005. These were amended in 2007. In buildings containing flats, working at a height is an important part of daily maintenance (such as window cleaning or changing light bulbs), and this is why the regulations are important to flat-owners.

A person can fall from even a small height and be injured. Indeed, the legislation simply defines a height as a place from which someone can be injured falling from it, even if it is at or below ground level. There is a duty on the landlord, managing agent, RMC and sometimes the flat-owner (if (s)he controls the work of others) to do all that is reasonably practical to prevent someone falling. This means that in the first instance working at a height must be avoided where possible. Where working at a height is necessary, the following should be noted:

- it should be properly planned, organised and supervised;

- the weather conditions should be considered, as well as places for emergency and rescue;

- those involved must be properly trained and competent;

- the equipment used must be appropriately inspected;

- measures must be taken to minimise distance and consequence of a fall should one occur (for example, through use of guard rails, safety harnesses, safety helmets);

- the place where the work is done must be safe;

- reasonable/practicable measures should be taken to prevent injury from anything falling from a height, such as being thrown or tipped or stored in such a way that its movement may cause injury. If this is not possible then the appropriate signage must be in place to warn people of the danger;

- employees must report any safety hazard to their employer and must be trained and use supplied equipment in the proper manner according to instructions.

The regulations apply to "work at any place", so as soon as a contractor or employee is on site, the law kicks in. Any work proposed should be risk-assessed by a competent person (see pp. 107-8) and a policy formulated to avoid injury. Proof of reasonable efforts made to avoid the risk will carry weight in the event of a problem. Ignorance of, for example, a contractor's proposed method will be no defence for the freeholder, RMC or managing agent.

For example, a recently reported incident concerned a small works contractor being instructed to carry out some work at first-floor level. While doing so, the instructing managing agent was reported to the Health and Safety Executive, although no accident whatsoever had actually taken place. Nevertheless, the Health and Safety Executive decided to investigate the matter in great detail with threats of prosecution, fines and jail sentences. The occurrence was reported by a concerned resident in the building opposite with no connection whatsoever to the building or managing agents in question. Further information can be found by contacting the Health and Safety Executive, the details of which are in the Appendix.

Lift testing

In addition to the inspections carried out under the engineering insurance policy, both passenger and goods lifts must be regularly maintained, and associated plant and equipment tested. This is because the landlord and those in the control of a building, such as the managing agent, have a legal duty to ensure that:

— the lifts there are safe to use, without risk to health;

— the lifts are properly maintained;

— the lifts are inspected and a risk assessment produced every six
   months by a competent person (often the insurers or their agents, who

are engineering surveyors);

– any issues, problems or hazards identified by the risk assessment are acted upon within a reasonable time.

The law is primarily contained in the Healthy and Safety at Work Act 1974, the EU Lift Directive 1995 and the Lifting Operations and Lifting Equipment Regulations 1998 (LOLER). The intention of these rules is to ensure that all existing lifts meet a minimum standard of safety, as mandated across the European Union. Most lifts installed before 1999 will not fully comply with the current safety standards.

The risk assessment will identify the level of risk associated with the lifts in the building, according to a standard scale of measurement: extreme/high/medium/low. Any identified item must be recorded in a formal report as prescribed by LOLER and a plan or timetable agreed by which time a remedy must be implemented. In circumstances where an extreme or high risk is identified, it is important to take immediate action to reduce the risk. This includes stopping the lift until the danger is removed. Practice guidelines suggest that extreme risks are dealt with immediately; high risks should be reduced within five years; medium risks within ten years; and low risks over a longer period. The LOLER report must be available for inspection for a minimum of two years or until the next report, whichever is the longer.

For further information, contact the Health and Safety Executive or the Safety Assessment Federation (whose details can be found in the Appendix to this book).

Control of Substances Hazardous to Health (COSHH)

It is a popular misconception that this does not apply to blocks of flats and only deals with large amounts of noxious chemicals in storage. This is not the case, and items such as the cleaning materials used in the common parts, the gardening chemicals and the method of carpet cleaning must be considered and risk-assessed. This duty still remains firmly with the landlord or the agent, who should be able to obtain the COSHH risk assessment from the contractor in question but, in the case of supplying the materials to directly employed cleaners/gardeners, must ensure that the risk is assessed by a competent person.

Disability discrimination

Strictly speaking, disability discrimination does not fall under the subject of health and safety. The Disability Discrimination Acts of 1995 and 2005 are intended to ensure that disabled persons are treated in exactly the same way as non-disabled persons, that no discrimination against the disabled takes place and that where reasonable adjustments to policies procedures, practices, aids and services can be implemented, they should be considered. The definition of "disability" covers a physical or mental impairment that has a substantial and long-term adverse effect on the ability to carry out normal day-to-day activities. As yet, there is no requirement to change physical aspects of a block, but no doubt case law will soon start to establish to what degree consideration has to be given and action taken. At the time of writing, careful consideration should be given to any application made by a disabled person, even if only concerned with the common areas of the block.

Reporting of Injuries, Diseases and Dangerous Occurrences Regulation (RIDDOR)

All injuries, diseases, accidents and work-related deaths must be reported to a national incident centre run by the Health and Safety Executive as a matter of law. This obligation is imposed on buildings containing flats and their managing agents by the Reporting of Injuries, Diseases and Dangerous Occurrences Regulations 1995 (RIDDOR). RIDDOR applies even if the injury does not affect directly employed staff but a contractor on site or a visiting member of the public. For further information see, www.riddor.gov.uk or telephone 0845 300 9923.

Houses in multiple occupation

The Management of Houses in Multiple Occupation (England) Regulations 2006, which were introduced pursuant to the Housing Act 2004, have caused some confusion with regard to flats. The legislation was intended to improve the standard of accommodation in the private rented sector, particularly at the lower end of the market. However, both individual flats and whole blocks can potentially be caught within the definition of a house in multiple occupation or "HMO". For example, one definition is of a building converted entirely into self-contained flats contrary to the standards of the 1991 Building Regulations and where more than one third of the flats are let on short-term tenancies. This definition could encompass a large percentage of blocks in this country. It is mandatory for an HMO to obtain a licence from the local authority. Licences can cost as much as £1000; failure to apply for a licence is a criminal offence and can result in a fine of up to £20,000. At the time of writing this book, the subject of HMOs and the licensing of HMOs is still uncertain, and different local authorities are reacting differently. The best advice would be to check with your local authority with regard to the circumstances of your particular block.

Summary

- Be safe, not sorry. When in doubt, do it, even if there is a cost implication . A small saving could prove to be an enormously false economy.

- Always ensure that persons employed to carry out risk assessments or undertake work are competent.

- Never assume that any particular building, however small, is exempt from any requirements where health and safety is concerned. It is not.

- Keep meticulous records – it may seem onerous but could potentially pay off in the long run.

09 MAINTENANCE CONTRACTS

Most blocks will have an element of on-site plant and equipment or require regular professional visits from, for example, a pest controller or water-safety engineer. This chapter examines the key maintenance contracts leaseholders should expect to find in their block.

What is a maintenance contract?

A maintenance contract is entered into for the servicing of plant or equipment testing and of course should be followed by a report of any defects noted for recommendations. These contracts are negotiated, usually by the managing agent and are influenced by budget, so ultimately you get what you pay for.

Maintenance contracts should be placed with a reliable, reputable and competent contractor who is preferably a member of a trade body. Often, prices are based on the equivalent of a three-tier service - that is the number of yearly visits, whether the contract would include replacement parts, call-out response times and so on. In the case of new equipment, the manufacturer will usually give a recommendation as to which type of contract is appropriate and suggest the level of service and frequency of visit deemed appropriate. Make sure the warranties are checked, since some warranties require a maintenance contract to be put in place on a specific basis, and the warranty is invalidated if this is not done. Other warranties include free maintenance for a year, but it is wise to check. While managing agents will hold copies of these contracts as a tool of the trade, it is recommended that a copy of all maintenance contracts is held on the site if this is at all possible.

Maintenance contract checklist

The following serves as a checklist for all items of plant and equipment that must have a regular maintenance contract covering them.

a) Lifts

The introduction of lifts into residential buildings contributed to a growth in the construction of tall residential structures. Today, the prevalence of lifts in blocks means they are often considered a necessity rather than a luxury. With a high proportion of residents, visitors and contractors using the lift in a block on a daily basis, it is important that lifts are properly maintained and safe to use. Lift maintenance can be an expensive item of expenditure for a block. Cared for regularly, a lift should give good use to a block. However, if not maintained properly or if mistreated, then the replacement costs and down time while not in use will be higher.

b) Boilers and associated plant

It is usual to find a communal boiler system or other associated plant in a block – for example, to provide communal hot water and heating to the building. This needs to be maintained so that it is safe to use and in good working order, particularly in winter months. Leaseholders also need to be aware of recent changes to the building regulations, which impact on the maintenance and installation of new boiler systems. The new regulations are in part motivated by environmental considerations and aim to make homes more energy efficient and produce fewer carbon dioxide emissions over a period of time.

c) Fire-safety systems

Recent changes to fire-safety regulations contained in the Regulatory Reform (Fire Safety) Order 2005 require blocks to undertake a fire-risk assessment. Risk of injury to people and damage to property in urban areas is particularly heightened where there is a high density of people living in close proximity. Therefore, it is only prudent that proper fire-safety precautions are in place and properly maintained. These can include appropriate exit signage, sprinkler systems, fire extinguishers, dry risers and fire-alarm systems.

d) Water testing

Many blocks have communal water systems, and these should be checked regularly to guard against waterborne diseases such as *Legionnella*.

e) Lightning conductors

Lightning conductors are more common in taller or more exposed residential blocks and consist of a piece of metal that will conduct electricity in the unfortunate event that the block is hit by a lightning strike. It is important that lightning conductors are regularly checked for their effectiveness. A direct hit from lightning, however rare, could cause a fire with potentially serious consequences for the building.

f) Eye bolts

Eye bolts can be found in different parts of a block, but one of the most common locations is on the outside of the building for use when carrying out maintenance or window cleaning. The contractor will attach a hoist and other necessary equipment to the eye bolt. If the eye bolt is not properly maintained, external maintenance will be a hazardous activity for which the block is responsible.

g) Fire extinguishers

There is no legal requirement to have fire extinguishers in the common parts of a block of flats. In fact, many fire brigades and fire officers have always avowed their intense dislike of fire extinguishers in blocks. They are not happy at the concept of untrained, concerned residents endeavouring to utilise fire extinguishers when they should be evacuating the building, not delaying to play with equipment untrained. If the block does have fire extinguishers (and it is now quite reasonable to suppose that some fire-safety risk assessments will recommend these, placing a different onus on the freeholder or agent), then the extinguishers must be under a maintenance - and - replacement contract. Training should be given to any persons likely to be involved in the use of the fire extinguishers, and it is prudent to have instructions displayed at prominent points.

h) Entry-phone systems and communal TV/satellite systems

It is not always necessary to have a maintenance contract on these (unless the systems are in place under a rental maintenance agreement). Normally, repairs can be carried out on an "as needed" basis.

i) Smoke detectors

Smoke detectors are considered by all the authorities to be highly desirable both in common parts and individual flats. These should be checked regularly and, where battery- or back-up battery operated, should have all batteries replaced at the same time.

j) Emergency lighting

It is recommended that back-up batteries be tested and the system operated at regular intervals batteries corrode if not utilised. Although this is not yet mandatory, it may become so.

k) Communal extractor-fan systems

It is prudent to have a regular maintenance contract on the extractors.

Summary

- Common sense dictates that any plant, equipment or installations should be maintained.

- Ensure that competent and reputable companies carry out the regular checks and maintenance procedures.

- In the case of new buildings, do not automatically assume that warranties will obviate the need for maintenance. Check the warranty agreements in the first instance; these will usually carry an obligation to maintain. Otherwise, the warranty in itself is invalidated.

- Do not book appointments for professional companies involved in abseiling or cradle window cleaning without ensuring that the requisite eye-bolt certificate is already in place and can be given to them prior to the site visit.

10 THE RIGHT-TO-MANAGE

All residential buildings containing flats, whatever their size and irrespective of their on-site facilities, require management of their common internal and external areas. The obligation of management is placed on the landlord by the lease, and a managing agent is often instructed to carry out the management tasks relating to the building. Since 2002, the law has provided flat-owners with the right to control the management of their building. Exercising the right-to-manage can be a relatively inexpensive and quick, no-fault solution for resolving existing management issues/disputes within a building. This chapter explains in outline the right-to-manage.

The responsibility of management

The most common reasons why the flat-owners in a building want to exercise the right-to-manage are because of unreasonably high service-charges or previous mismanagement of the building. However, taking on control of the management of the building also carries with it serious responsibilities, and so flat-owners should consider their options carefully before embarking on exercising their right-to-manage. Once the right-to-manage has been exercised, the right-to-manage will step into the firing line in respect of any dissatisfaction regarding future management of the building. In addition, the directors of the right-to-manage will also need to comply with a complex web of legislation regarding property management and company law. Sometimes, flat-owners will feel that the benefit of being able to manage their own affairs outweighs these responsibilities. However, depending on the reasons why right-to-manage is sought, other solutions may be more appropriate – such as buying the freehold or making an application to the leasehold valuation tribunal (LVT) for the appointment of a manager.

In respect of the right-to-manage, Section 96(5) of the Commonhold and Leasehold Reform Act 2002 makes clear that the "management functions" expected of a right-to-manage company relate to the services, repairs, maintenance, improvements, insurance and management of the building. In practice, this will include things such as looking after the lifts and other plant and machinery in the building, arranging insurance, collecting service-charges, providing caretakers/porters and so on. The right-to-manage company (RTM co) will also be responsible for granting the various consents (usually by way of a licence) required under the lease before certain action can be taken by the flat-owners. This will include, for example, consent to make internal alterations to individual flats, to sublet or to assign a lease.

Qualification

The right-to-manage is not available to all buildings. To qualify, the building must satisfy the following conditions; set out in Section 72 of the Commonhold and Leasehold Reform Act (CLARA) 2002:

- the building must be self-contained; or be part of a building that is self-contained (see legislation);

- the building must include at least two flats, and

- two thirds of the flats must be let to "qualifying tenants" (that is, flat-owners whose lease when granted is for a term exceeding 21 years);

- any non-residential part of the premises must not exceed 25 per cent of the total floor area;

In circumstances where there is a single development of several individual buildings, each building would need to qualify separately for the right-to-manage and make their own applications for the right-to-manage.

Exercise of the right

The right-to-manage cannot be exercised by individual leaseholders, but by a special company identified by Section 73-74 of CLARA 2002 as a RTM Co. This is because, over the lifetime of the building, the identity of the individual flat-owners may change, but the company will remain constant and provide continuity of the management function. In order for the RTM Co to exercise the right-to-manage, at least 50 per cent of the qualifying tenants in the building must be members of the company. However, there is no minimum requirement of qualifying tenants to form the company initially (which can be done with the assistance of a solicitor or company formation agent).

RTM Cos are subject to certain statutory requirements. For example, they must be limited by guarantee and adopt a Memorandum and Articles of Association, as set out in the RTM Cos (Memorandum and Articles of

Association) (England) Regulations 2003. In other respects, an RTM Co is subject to the same rules and regulations as all companies registered at Companies House.

Gathering support

In order for the RTM Co to be effective in its purpose, enough qualifying leaseholders must become members. This will require a concerted and determined effort on behalf of one or more qualifying tenants in order to create a groundswell of support for the RTM Co By law, all qualifying flat-owners must be invited to become members of the RTM Co (see Section 78 of CLARA 2002). There is a prescribed form of notice inviting participation which must be served on all qualifying flat-owners containing:

− a statement that the RTM Co intends to acquire the right-to-manage;

− the names of the members of the RTM Co;

− the purpose of the RTM Co;

− an invitation to qualifying flat-owners to become members of the RTM Co, and the implications of joining;

− the names of the directors and company secretary of the RTM Co;

− the names of the landlord and any other person who is party to the lease other than the lessees;

− the registered number of the RTM Co;

− the address of the registered office of the RTM Co;

− a copy of the Memorandum and Articles of Association or a statement explaining where these documents can be located.

The purpose of the RTM Co will be to acquire the ability to determine the management functions of the building from the landlord (except for any flats owned by the landlord or any commercial space). As a consequence, the RTM Co can then decide:

— to keep the current managing agent;

— to replace the current managing agent with another professional managing agent;

— to self-manage the building (in which case, management experience of the members of the company should be explained);

In addition, although it is not compulsory, it is useful to provide a draft plan/budget to show prospective members how the RTM Co intends to manage the building after the right has been exercised.

Because each member of the company will be liable for the landlord's costs from the time the initial notice is served until the right is exercised, it is important that participation in the company is carefully considered and, where appropriate, the flat-owner receives independent legal advice (see Section 88–89 of the 2002 Act). Once a flat-owner has decided to become a member, they should respond to the notice inviting participation, whereupon they will be inscribed in the company's records and be issued with appropriate corporate certification.

Unless the notice inviting participation is carefully drafted to include the above information and served properly, it may be considered to be invalid. Therefore, it is prudent for the company itself to obtain its own legal advice at the earliest opportunity, since this will avoid any later potential challenge by the landlord.

Before exercising the right

Before exercising the right-to-manage, the RTM Co should make a thorough investigation of the existing management arrangements for the building. This may require the involvement of a professional managing agent or chartered surveyor to advise the RTM Co on management issues on a consultancy basis even if they are not later retained as the managing agent for the building.

Much of this management information will already be known by the flat-owners or be available from public sources such as the Land Registry. However, if the information is unclear or otherwise unknown, then the flat-owners have a right to request the information either under the Landlord and Tenant Act 1985 or Section 82 of CLARA 2002. In the former case, the landlord will have 21 days to respond; in the latter case, he will have 28 days. Furthermore, under Section 83 of the 2002 Act, the RTM Co has the right to demand access after service of the notice of claim for "any person authorised" by the RTM Co to "any part of the premises if that is reasonable" in connection with the claim. This will enable the RTM Co, for example, to inspect plant and machinery (such as, lifts), as well as the fabric of the building in order to understand the management, repair and renovation issues involved following the exercise of the right.

If, even after extensive research, the details of the landlord or other parties to the lease cannot be found, then an application to the leasehold valuation tribunal for an order entitling the RTM Co to acquire the right can be made.

The notice of claim

The right-to-manage is formally exercised by the RTM Co by serving a notice of claim on the landlord, each qualifying tenant and any other parties named on the lease no fewer than 14 days after the service of notice inviting participation. Under the Right-to-Manage (Prescribed Particulars and Forms) (England) Regulations 2003, the notice of claim must be in writing and state the following key points:

- the building and the grounds on which it qualifies for the right-to-manage;

- the full names and addresses of each qualifying flat-owner who is also a member of the RTM Co (and details of their leases to verify their ability to qualify);

- the name and registered office of the RTM Co;

- the date by which a counter-notice should be served (no less than one month after the service of the notice of claim);

- the date on which the RTM Co intends to acquire the right-to-manage (at least three months after service of the counter-notice);

It is important to understand that the right-to-manage is exercised on a no-fault basis, and it is the absence of the apportionment of blame that often makes right-to-manage an attractive route to solving management problems in a building.

The counter-notice

The landlord may serve a counter-notice by the date specified in the notice of claim. The counter-notice should either:

- admit that the RTM Co is entitled to acquire the right-to-manage; or;

- deny that the RTM Co is entitled to acquire the right-to-manage (giving reasons).

If the landlord admits right-to-manage, then the management passes to the RTM Co on the date specified. If the right-to-manage is disputed, then the matter should be decided by the leasehold valuation tribunal.

This requires the RTM Co to make an application within two months of the landlord's counter-notice (see Section 84(3) - (8) of the 2002 Act). Otherwise, the claim for the right-to-manage is deemed to be withdrawn (Section 87 of the 2002 Act).

The landlord only has limited technical grounds on which to challenge entitlement to the right-to-manage (see Section 84(2)(b) of the 2002 Act). These are:

– the building does not qualify; or

– the RTM Co does not comply with the legislative requirements; or

– the members of the RTM Co do not represent 50 per cent of the flats in the building

Note that the landlord does not have the same rights to information given to the RTM Co and must make his or her own independent investigations from his or her own records of the leases and publicly available information (such as the records at Companies House).

If no counter-notice is served, then it is deemed that the landlord accepts the request for the right-to-manage.

Acquiring the management

Once the landlord has accepted the right-to-manage by the RTM Co, or it has been determined by the LVT in favour of the RTM Co, then the management will be acquired on the "acquisition date" (Section 90 of the 2002 Act). At this point, the landlord (and any other parties to the lease) will become full members of the RTM Co If there are several landlords or other parties to the lease, then the Memorandum and Articles of Association provide a mechanism to ensure that the flat-owners cannot be outvoted on company decisions.

As soon as possible after receiving the notice of claim, and no later than the "determination date" (the date by which the counter-notice must be served), the landlord should serve:

- a notice on all appointed contractors, explaining that that the right-to-manage the building is to be acquired by an RTM Co and providing its details and a statement advising the contractors to contact the RTM Co if they wish to be retained;

- a notice on the RTM Co particularising each existing contract, the details of the appropriate contractor in each case and a statement advising the RTM Co to contact those contractors it wishes to retain.

This is provided for in Section 92 of the 2002 Act.

Also, any service-charges collected but unused, reserve-fund or sinking-fund trust accounts must be transferred to the control of the RTM Co further to Section 94 of the 2002 Act. There may be difficulty in identifying the exact sum in question. In such circumstances (and assuming the amount in question cannot be agreed between the parties), an application can be made to the LVT to determine the issue. In any situation, prudence suggests that an independent audit of the relevant accounts will be useful, and it is always helpful if the landlord agrees to make an interim payment of the undisputed amount to help the cash flow of the fledgling RTM Co.

Once the management has passed to the RTM Co, it has a duty to the landlord not to mismanage the building in such a way as to reduce the value of the landlord's interest in the building. This is because the right-to-manage only transfers the power of management, while the ownership of the building and the individual flats remains unaffected. The landlord remains responsible for his covenants under the lease (see Chapter 1), such as quiet enjoyment and non-derogation from grant.

The landlord and the RTM Co will also have to cooperate on certain issues. For example, when approval is required by a flat-owner under the lease (for example, to make alterations), this can be granted by the RTM Co but the landlord must be informed within a statutory prescribed time limit (Section 98(4) Commonhold and Leasehold Reform Act 2002). In the case of an approval relating to assignment, underletting, charging, parting with possession, the making of structural alterations or improvements/alterations of use, 30 days' notice must be given. In all other cases, 14 days' notice must be provided to the landlord. The landlord can object to the proposed consent being granted by notifying the RTM Co and the relevant flat-owner. If an agreement between the parties cannot be reached, then an application to the leasehold valuation tribunal will need to be made by any of the parties to decide the matter.

In situations where there has been a breach of a lease covenant by a flat-owner (such as making an alteration without approval or failure to pay service-charges), the RTM Co has a statutory duty to ensure that the breach is remedied (see Section 100(2) of the 2002 Act). If the breach is not remedied, then the landlord will need to be informed because the remedy of forfeiture cannot be exercised by the RTM Co (see Section 100 (3) of the 2002 Act).

Ending the right-to-manage

The right-to-manage lasts for an indefinite amount of time. However, Section 105 of the Commonhold and Leasehold Reform Act provides that the right may be terminated for the following reasons:

– by agreement with the landlord;

– if the RTM Co enters receivership, voluntary insolvency, is struck off or wound up;

– if a manager is appointed under Part 2 of the Landlord and Tenant Act

1987. This will be because either the landlord or the RTM Co are in breach of the lease, demand unreasonable service-charges or fail to comply with an approved code of management practice.

If the right-to-manage is terminated, then no further application for the right-to-manage can be made within four years, without the consent of the LVT.

Summary

- The right-to-manage is a no-fault procedure provided by statute enabling flat-owners to take over the management of their building.

- The right-to-manage is exercised by an RTM Co on behalf of all participating flat-owners, and not by the flat-owners acting on an individual basis.

- There are certain qualifying criteria for the establishiment of the RTM Co and its members, so the legislation must be carefully checked.

- The procedure is relatively straightforward and involves the RTM Co serving a notice on the landlord requesting the right-to-manage. The landlord is given a limited opportunity to respond by way of counter-notice.

- Once the right-to-manage has been acquired, the RTM Co controls the management function of the building along with all the rights and responsibilities that go with it.

11 THE COMPANY

As a leaseholder there are many companies you
may come across concerning your building, such as
a resident management company, right-to-manage
company, or commonhold company. Therefore, it is
useful to understand the legal status of a company and
the different types of company in the flat sector.

© www.newsontheblock.com

What is a company?

A company can be distinguished from other forms of organisation,
such as partnership or sole trader, by the fact that it has a separate and
distinct legal identity to its members as well as limited liability. In law, a
company is considered to be a legal "person". This means that it can sue
and be sued, own property and make contractual decisions.

The actions a company takes are a reflection of its members (also called "shareholders"), and in particular its board of directors. All private limited companies must have a minimum of one director and a company secretary (though this requirement will no longer be mandatory following the Companies Act 2007). The director and company secretary together form the board of directors. The board of directors is responsible for the management of the company. This is discussed further in Chapter 9.

There are two types of limited company: companies limited by shares, and companies limited by guarantee. Where a company is limited by shares, limited liability means that the shareholders are not liable for a sum greater than their paid-up share capital. In simple terms, providing the shareholder has paid the amount due for its share(s) in the company, no creditor can demand any further payment from them. Companies can also be limited by guarantee. Instead of shareholders, the guarantors (members) are only liable for the amount they have agreed to contribute towards its assets on winding up (usually £1). Also, companies limited by guarantee may not distribute their profits to their members. Right-to-manage and commonhold-association companies often incorporate as companies limited by guarantee. Limited liability is a useful legal device for providing people with a form of protection against the risks of commercial enterprise. The benefit of this for buildings containing flats will be apparent from reading the following pages.

The characteristics of a company as a form of organisation make it an ideal vehicle to use in respect of blocks of flats. There are two principal types of company you may encounter in a block of flats: the resident management company (RMC) and the right-to-manage company. Both of these are explained further below.

Resident management company

The original RMC, may be the company set up by the developer/ freeholder on a new development. All the lessees of the building are compulsory members. The company may be limited either by shares or by guarantee. The purpose of the original RMC is usually to take on the obligations of the freeholder and manage the property either directly or by appointing managing agents. Commonly, the RMC may have a lease over the common areas granted by the freeholder. In these cases, the RMC is not just a "manager" but also has a vested interest in part of the property. New purchasers in a development are frequently in doubt as to whether there actually is a resident management company and whether they are part of it. To resolve any ambiguity, the lease should be consulted, since this will list the relevant parties, and a search at Companies House will demonstrate the control of the RMC.

An RMC is not treated any differently in law to any other company. The RMC must file an annual return, submit annual accounts (within the prescribed period of ten months from the financial year end for filing in Companies House) and is under all the usual obligations applicable under company law. The RMC also requires the statutory number of officers in order to remain in existence. If found operating either insolvently or without these officers, the RMC can be struck off, and its assets revert to the Treasury solicitor. If this unfortunate consequence happens, it may be necessary to set up a new company and transfer all the assets of the struck off RMC into the new company with agreement by the Treasury solicitor. In some cases and subject to agreement by the Treasury solicitor, it is possible to revive the original RMC. There are costs involved in either remedy.

Right-to-manage company

Since 2003, provisions contained in the Commonhold and Leasehold Reform Act 2002 enable a block of flats to take control of the management of their own building. Further detail on the right-to-manage is explained in Chapter 10 of this book. However, for present purposes it is sufficient to understand that an element of the right-to-manage process involves the block forming a dedicated company responsible for the management of the block. This company is called a right-to-manage company (RTM co). All participating leaseholders become shareholders in the company. Although an RTM Co is set up with different rights, ultimately it has the same responsibilities as an RMC.

Commonhold association company

The commonhold association is a creature of statute, namely the Commonhold and Leasehold Reform Act 2002. The purpose of the company is to own and manage the common parts. All the flat-owners become members of the commonhold association. To date, there are few commonhold association companies in existence.

Memorandum and Articles of Association

The Memorandum and Articles of Association (Mem and Arts) are the essential constitutional documents for the company. These documents set out the purpose and function of the company and will stipulate, for example, whether directors retire by rotation, the general procedures for the election of directors, conduct of annual general meetings, voting procedures, removal of directors, and the minimum and maximum number of directors required for proceedings to be quorate (as opposed to the number of officers required for the company to remain in existence under company law).

Some of the content of the Memorandum and Articles of Association can be changed by resolution. This can be particularly useful in cases of archaic memorandums not particularly geared to companies relevant to the flat sector. Any resolution must be recorded as a minute and lodged at Companies House as a formal resolution.

The Memorandum and Articles of Association will dictate the objects of the company. Therefore, it is important that they reflect what the company does. Sometimes, when companies are first incorporated or bought "off the shelf" from a companies formation bureaux they have been set up with a standard set of constitutional documents. It is advisable that these are reviewed and changed, where appropriate, to reflect the true activities and running of the company.

In the case of a RTM co, there is a prescribed set of Memorandum and Articles of Association that are, of course, very strictly relevant to the control of the maintenance and management of the property. By contrast, it is quite common to find a very wide-ranging set of objects in an RMC, covering investing, borrowing, mortgaging and various activities not actually relevant to the management/maintenance. Sometimes, the Memorandum and Articles of Association of an RTM Co can be adapted to suit an existing RMC and adopted via resolution, as described above.

In all other respects, an RMC must function like any commercial trading company and adhere to its Memorandum and Articles of Association and company law. The responsibilities of an RMC are to ensure the prudent management of the block, whether delegated or self-managed, and to adhere to all legislation covering the same.

Statutory registers and books

The registers and books comprise a list of the past and present shareholders of the company, minutes of meetings of the company, copies of the accounts and a company sea. These must be maintained, usually by the company secretary, and should be held at the registered office of the company. These documents are in the public domain and should be available for inspection by the shareholders of the company. It is worth noting that the minutes of the annual general meetings form part of the statutory documents and, as such, should be restricted to formal corporate matters. The minutes should be recorded in a formal format and exclude irrelevant debate among irate leaseholders (for example, references to Mrs A objecting to a remark by Mr B etc).

Appointment of directors and officers

Usually, every private limited company must have at least one director, under the age of 70, who is (re-)elected on an annual basis at an AGM. The requirement for a company secretary is likely to change in the proposed Company law-reform. Nevertheless, the Memorandum and Articles of Association must be consulted to discover the circumstances and procedures by which directors and officers can be appointed and under what circumstances.

Responsibilities and functions of the company

In broad terms, the RMC or RTM Co is effectively a vehicle for carrying out the management and maintenance responsibilities of a building containing flats and representing the interests of the members of the company.

Shareholders

The body of shareholders of an RMC or RTM Co are commonly comprised of the lessees of the block concerned. Each flat in the block ought to have one share in the company. This is not always the case. The body of shareholders will elect officers to represent their interest and collectively empower these directors to represent them and make decisions for them. If dissatisfied with this representation, the shareholders can elect additional directors, remove existing directors or vote against resolutions as circumstances dictate and subject to the contents of the Memorandum and Articles of Association.

In cases where the company is limited by guarantee rather than by shares, the lessees are "members" rather than shareholders and will hold a certificate of membership rather than a share certificate.

Company law reform

At the time of writing, changes to company law are being introduced, which will affect the types of company discussed here. Leaseholders should check the effect of these reforms on their circumstances.

Summary

- It is of the utmost importance always to check the Memorandum and Articles of Association of the company.

- Remember, the Memorandum and Articles of Association can be changed through the proper procedures.

- It is not compulsory to have a directors and officers indemnity insurance policy in place, but it is certainly prudent, both for the volunteer directors in an RMC and as comfort to anyone wishing to take action against the directors.

- In an RMC where all lessees are members and the company solely exists to administer the management/maintenance of the building, the cost of a D&O policy should, subject to suitable provisions in the lease, be a recoverable cost through the service-charge. Ideally, resident management companies, as freeholders or head leaseholders or RTM Cos where not all lessees are participants should have auditors apportion the costs of such items as D&O policies, audit fee, filing fees etc between the corporate expenditure and the service-charge expenditure. However, in other respects, company expenses are not within the definition of a service-charge under Section 18 of the Landlord and Tenant Act 1985.

- The managing agents, where appointed, will take instructions from the directors of the RMC, and these instructions should be carried out, presuming that they are lawful. Assuming these instructions are lawful, members of the company, if dissatisfied with the instructions of their elected officers, should take issue with the elected officers rather than with the managing agents. Equally, of course, managing agents should refuse to carry out any instructions from the directors in an RMC that are not lawful.

- Any conflict of interest must be declared by an officer of the RMC.

- Most Memorandum and Articles of Association for RMCs will stipulate that the officers are volunteers at no remuneration, some will make provisions for the appointment of expert, professional officers who can be paid, but this is relatively unusual in RMC companies. It is generally not considered either desirable or prudent for elected officers from the available lessees to be paid for their time. Equally it may be desirable to hire professional help, although this is usually in a non-voting capacity and more of a guidance role.

12 DIRECTORS & OFFICERS

As a leaseholder, there are many companies you may come across concerning your building, such as a resident management company, right-to-manage-company, or commonhold company. Therefore, it is useful to understand the legal status of a company and the different types of company in the flat sector.

© www.newsontheblock.com

Directors

All private limited companies must have at least one director (two in the case of a public limited company). The names and addresses of the company directors (collectively known as the board of directors) and any changes to them must be kept at the registered office of the company and also duly filed at companies house, where they are available for public inspection. This is because the details of the directors of a company are a matter of public record.

Appointment

The procedure for the appointment and removal of company directors is prescribed in the Articles of Association. The Articles of Association will prescribe, for example, the ability to co-opt, to appoint alternate directors or for directors to retire by rotation and offer themselves for re-election. There will also be provisions to determine the minimum/maximum number of directors and how many are required to be present in order to be quorate for any major decisions. Although directors do not, by law, need to be shareholders, with regard to resident management companies (RMCs) this is commonly the case and it is prudent for the Articles of Association so to provide. A director of an RMC will be more effective if (s)he has a vested interest in the block, and where shareholding is made a prerequisite, the director must take up such shareholding within two months of the appointment. There are no formal qualifications required to be a company director, but careful consideration should be given as to who is appointed a director. The efficient running of the RMC will not be helped by those of disreputable character or physical or mental incapacity. Subject to alternative provisions in the Articles of Association, a person aged 70 or over cannot be appointed as a director, and any existing director reaching that age must retire. Irrespective of provisions contained in the Articles of Association, a director can be removed by ordinary resolution.

Duties

A company director will be expected to run the business of the company for its members and is thus in a fiduciary position with the company. This means that a director is expected to comply with the strictest standard of behaviour, commonly expressed as duties of care, skill and loyalty owed to the company. In practice, a director must disclose any conflict of interest arising, not make any secret profit out of his position as director and generally exercise his role as director in the interests of the company, carefully, honestly and in good faith. Directors of a RMCs have the same responsibilities and liabilities as directors of large multinational organisations.

In circumstances where there has been a breach of duty by a director, it will be a decision for the company whether to ratify the wrong or take legal action against the director. No individual shareholder can sue a director for breach of duty, because the director owes the duty to the company alone. The company itself must bring the action, or the shareholder on behalf of the company.

There have been cases where directors of RMC companies have expressed a cavalier attitude to the apparent conflict between their role as a company director and their self-interest in the block. For example, there is a case of a block where a director refused to pay the service-charge and then prevented the RMC taking legal action to recover the arrears.

Liability and insurance

Directors are subject to individual and personal liability, as well as collective liability with their fellow directors. This is sometimes referred to as "joint and several liability". The issue of directors' and officers' indemnity insurance cover has already been covered in detail in Chapter 4. Although there is no legal requirement for directors' and officers' insurance, it is certainly worth having not only to protect those individual in serving positions, but also to provide an additional degree of comfort for third parties contracting with the company.

There are many examples of litigious disputes involving directors of RMCs. One case involved a disgruntled lessee who forced the local council to prosecute the RMC for failure to comply with a Section 20 notice. The prosecution was aborted at the 11th hour due to a sudden

spurt of activity culminating in compliance with the Section 20 notice. However, all directors of the RMC resigned immediately thereafter, not wishing to undergo such an ordeal and the associated potential liability ever again. This case illustrates the level of responsibility and strict standards of compliance by which directors of RMCs can be held to account. This degree of accountability can dissuade many well-meaning lessees from becoming directors of their RMC. If an insufficient number of directors volunteer, then the RMC is impossible to run effectively, and this, in turn, affects the whole block. Therefore, a balance must be reached between holding directors to account and scaring potential directors from
holding office.

The chairman

The chairman of the board of directors is elected by the directors and not the shareholders, as sometimes thought. The chairman's role is to lead the board of directors in conducting the business of the company. This includes chairing any meetings, marshalling any discussion and encouraging the directors to reach a consensus on decision-making. In blocks of flats, where contentious issues can often lead to emotional debate, the chairman must possess the seemingly impossible combination of patience, diplomacy and authority. The Articles of Association will dictate the provisions of a chairman's casting vote when appropriate.

The treasurer

Although the position of treasurer is commonly found in a residents' association (because of their constitution and the necessity to deal with the funds voluntarily contributed), most RMCs do not have the same position. In practise, most RMCs receive funds either in their capacity as landlords or as leaseholders, and not as voluntary donations. This includes ground rent and other income collected and accounted for on behalf of the RMC by their managing agents or accountants/solicitors. Service-charge funds are not corporate income.

Nevertheless, it is advisable to have a director designated as the "finance director" (especially where the relevant expertise is available), to liaise on all financial matters with the appointed managing agents or board of directors.

The company secretary

The company secretary is an officer of the company. In small private companies, the company secretary can also be a director. At present, all companies must have a company secretary, although this requirement is likely to be changed when the new company law comes into force (see below). The company secretary is appointed by the directors.

In contrast to directors, the company secretary of a public company must satisfy certain prerequisites before being considered for the role. The company secretary must be a professional (accountant, charted secretary, solicitor, barrister) or the directors must be satisfied that the person is capable of carrying out the functions of secretary. While in the case of RMCs (which are normally private limited companies) these prerequisites do not apply, where possible it is advantageous to apply these criteria when selecting a company secretary.

The company secretary is responsible for the administrative duties of the company. These include registering all forms at Companies House, ensuring share transfer or membership certificates are completed, the upkeep of the statutory books for the company, signing the AGM notices, taking the minutes of meetings and ensuring the annual return is submitted to Companies House. Due to the level of administration and the technical nature of this position, many RMCs choose to appoint a specialist company secretarial service to fulfil this role rather than one of their fellow lessees. It is always worth investigating whether your managing agent or accountant can offer a company secretarial service; otherwise there are several independent agencies worth approaching.

Change of directors or officers

There will be circumstances where the directors and officers need to be changed. The procedure for changing the director or officer of an RMC is contained in the Articles of Association, subject to company law.

A director can be removed by "ordinary resolution" of the shareholders of the company before his/her term of office has expired. This requires putting a resolution under a special notice and, on members' requisition, calling an extraordinary general meeting. The members requisition should be composed of not less than one tenth of the voting take-up capital of the company (in the case of a company limited by guarantee not shares, members representing not less than one tenth of the total voting rights). The legal detail on this issue is beyond the scope of this book, save to say that it is possible to remove a director if the will exists.

Another particular concern to RMCs are the circumstances where a director or officer sells their flat and decides (understandably) not to continue in their previous corporate role. It can be particularly difficult to find suitable replacements, and the consequence of having no volunteers has already been described separately.

From an administrative viewpoint, in an RMC a change of directors/officers can happen with monotonous regularity as lessees sell and buy flats in the block. Whether it is the company secretary, an administrator of the same, or a volunteer director or nominee, it should be ensured that requisite forms are lodged with Companies House and also that the proposing, seconding and consent forms, together with the official resignation letters giving applicable dates for resignation are retained within the company's documents.

Communications

Communications between directors are extremely important. Regular meetings at monthly or quarterly intervals are recommended. These should be run by the chairman of the board in a formal fashion, with an agenda circulated in advance and minutes recorded for distribution afterwards. Sometimes, it may be useful to invite the property manager of the block to these meetings. Any decisions taken at these meetings should be on the basis of being quorate.

On a practical level, care should be taken to avoid instances where one volunteer director or officer single-mindedly pursues an issue and thereafter fails to attend meetings and provide input and response to communications between directors. The role of director is subject to fiduciary obligations and should not be hijacked for personal gain (financial or otherwise). Such individuals may become more of a hindrance to the board and should be encouraged to resign. Some Memorandums and Articles of Association will include the proviso that non-attendance at a minimum number of meetings is grounds for removal.

The issue of directors communicating with the shareholders is a particularly controversial one in the RMC situation, where people are concerned about their flat and the block in general. For example, distributing minutes of board meetings to shareholders is sometimes viewed as an invitation for unnecessary and time-consuming aggravation if shareholders respond. However, lessee-shareholders often do want to know what is going on in their block, and it is good practice to keep them informed, providing a suitable balance can be achieved between the provision of information and not overburdening the board with time-consuming responses. Many RMCs decide that, aside from the company law requirements of an annual general meeting, communication with shareholders should be restricted to a general newsletter and ad hoc notices.

RMC directors' and officers' remuneration

The generally accepted rule is that directors and officers are acting in the best interests of their own and their neighbours' investments and, as such, are unpaid, unrewarded and unthanked volunteers. The potential for serious conflict of interests/pecuniary advantage is therefore removed. However, as property management becomes a more complex and regulated task and the necessity for qualified expertise essential, it would not be surprising if, in the future, remuneration for running an RMC becomes the norm.

The Memorandum and Articles of Association for the company should be consulted to confirm the position on remuneration provisions, as well as the lease for recoverable costs under the service-charge provision.

Summary

- Check your Memorandum and Articles of Association.

- Check your lease in relation to recoverable costs.

- Separate your corporate accounts from your service-charge accounts.

- Election of directors and officers is a serious issue, and apathy should not rule. Communicate and encourage interested parties to vote.

- Members of RMCs who have no desire to participate and be proactive should desist from finding the easier option of heckling from the back benches, and put themselves forward for election.

- The law and Memorandum and Articles of Association will allow the removal of undesirable directors and officers.

- Do communicate as directors and officers with the members of the company you are representing.

- The remuneration of volunteer directors and officers who have a vested interest in the investment in the property is not desirable.

13 COMPANY, BOARD & RESIDENTS' ASSOCIATION MEETINGS

Blocks of flats that have a resident management company will need to know how to call, run and report meetings of the company and its board of directors. This is because a Resident management company is treated no differently to any other company – all have to conform with the companies legislation currently in force. However, even in blocks where there is no resident management company and perhaps only an informal residents' association, it is worth noting some of the procedures in this chapter. Even as a residents' association, it is worth emulating certain elements of company meetings to aid the efficient running of your organisation. The important contribution effective meetings have to the efficient running of the block should not be underestimated. Some blocks suffer because directors/committee members are not fully aware of what is expected. This chapter outlines the requirements placed on a company with regard to holding meetings.

The Annual general meeting

Under the Companies Act 1985, every company (whether limited by shares or guarantee) must hold an annual general meeting (AGM) every year. Some companies may elect to dispense with the requirement of an AGM. The meeting is for directors, officers and shareholders of the company. There is an exception for newly formed companies, which have 18 months from the date of first incorporation in which to hold an AGM. Otherwise, if more than 15 months expire without the holding of an AGM, then the directors and officers of the company are liable to a fine.

A common misconception is that the AGM is an opportunity for the company to discuss (and often debate) all the issues of the block relating to the past year. This is incorrect – the AGM has a specific purpose. The AGM is simply the statutory time when the accounts are presented to the shareholders, directors and auditors are (re)appointed, and the remuneration of the auditors approved. The purpose of the AGM is to inject an element of democracy into the company by enabling the shareholders to question the directors on the accounts and the company's financial position. Although some lessee-directors try to run the RMC as their own personal fiefdom, the AGM is an opportunity for the shareholders to curtail any over exuberance. Many blocks choose the time of an AGM as an opportunity to discuss the issues concerning the block in general. Strictly speaking, the AGM should be formally closed as a meeting once the statutory business has been conducted. Any further discussion about the block can then continue immediately afterwards.

Every shareholder, director and auditor must be given 21 days' notice in writing in advance of the AGM. However, a shorter notice period can be agreed among the members providing such agreement is unanimous. The notice must contain the following information:

– that the meeting being called is an AGM;

- the date, time and place of the AGM;

- the business to be conducted at the AGM, including any resolutions that are being proposed;

- that a shareholder may appoint a proxy to attend and vote on his behalf at the meeting.

It is advised that any background information concerning the business of the meeting (for example, a copy of the accounts) is circulated with the AGM notice. From the information provided, the shareholder must be able to decide whether it is in his interest to attend the meeting, but it is not obligatory to do so. Also, note that the accidental omission to notify any shareholder or non-receipt of the notice calling the AGM does not invalidate the proceedings.

The extraordinary general meeting

Any meeting other than an AGM is termed an extraordinary general meeting (EGM). Unlike an AGM, an EGM only requires 14 days' notice in writing (unless a special resolution of the company is being considered). A shorter notice period can be agreed by shareholders holding a majority of 95 per cent of the votes in the company.

Proxies

Any shareholder who could otherwise attend and vote at a general meeting can appoint another person as his proxy to attend, vote and speak at the meeting instead of him. The proxy does not have to be a shareholder in the company. It is usual practice for the company to provide shareholders with a proxy form with the notice of the meeting. The proxy form should be completed and returned in advance of the meeting.

Quorum

For the AGM to be valid, and for any resolutions considered to be validly passed, the meeting must be quorate. This requires there to be in attendance a minimum of two shareholders of the company who are entitled to vote.

Voting

In most cases, voting is conducted by a show of hands. Every shareholder has one vote, which can be exercised on a show of hands. Proxies cannot vote on a show of hands must but present their vote in writing. Sometimes, rather than taking a vote on a show of hands, a poll may be taken (see the Articles of Association for more detail). In these circumstances, every shareholder has one vote per share owned.

The minutes

Formal minutes of the AGM should be taken and recorded, usually by the company secretary. Following the meeting, the minutes should be circulated among the directors, shareholders and auditors for any amendments. An approved set of minutes should be signed and dated by the chairman of the board of directors. The signed set of minutes should be kept with the company's books.

Resolutions of the company

Resolutions express the decision-making power of the company. There are three types of resolution:

— **Ordinary resolutions:** These are the most common type of resolution and are passed by a simple majority of members entitled to vote at a meeting. Ordinary resolutions only need to be filed at Companies House in limited circumstances.

— **Special resolutions:** These are normally required for changes to the constitution of the company. Special resolutions require a majority of

75 per cent of members entitled to vote at a meeting. In addition, once passed, special resolutions must be filed at Companies House.

- **extraordinary resolutions:** Rarely used, except for modifying share classes or winding up the company, extraordinary resolutions also require a 75 per cent majority of members entitled to vote at a meeting. The difference between an extraordinary resolution and a special resolution is that there is no notice requirement.

- **elective resolutions:** In the case of a resident management company (RMC), an elective resolution is commonly used to dispense with the holding of an annual general meeting or the annual appointment of auditors. Elective resolutions require 100 per cent agreement among the shareholders entitled to vote at a meeting.

- If a resolution is required to be filed at Companies House and this is not done within 15 days, then the company may be liable to a fine.

The board meeting & block management committee meeting

Most of the day-to-day running of the company is conducted through regular board meetings of the directors. Many blocks choose to hold these meetings at the same time as their regular block management committee meetings.

Board meetings are more informal than general meetings of the company and are not subject to any formal notice or filing requirements. Nevertheless, it is good practice to circulate an agenda prior to the meeting. The chairman of the board should run the meeting, and the company secretary (or one of the directors where this function is out-sourced) should keep the minutes. Minutes should be circulated and approved after the meeting is closed. If the probity of the directors is ever called into question, these records will be useful evidence.

Block management committee meetings are different from board meetings because they should only consider issues relating to the block rather than the RMC itself. There is sometimes a fine line between the two. Where possible, it is advantageous for the property manager for the block to attend these committee meetings. Issues relating to the block can then be discussed effectively and proper instructions provided. As with board meetings and general meetings, committee meetings should be called in advance with an agenda and a copy of the previous meeting's minutes attached. Each block decides on the most appropriate time intervals between which to hold committee meetings, but to run a block efficiently it is recommended that monthly or bimonthly meetings are held.

Because these meetings will inevitably be between neighbours who are also shareholders in the block, there may be a temptation for formalities to be overlooked, and it is important for the chairman to maintain an element of decorum regarding these meetings. Some blocks choose to use the opportunity of a meeting as a social gathering between neighbours, but this should always be left until after the business of the meeting has been concluded. It is acceptable and sometimes important to conduct a healthy debate about issues on the agenda to reach a committee decision, but this should always be done in a polite and respectful manner. Remember, you also have to live in close proximity to your neighbouring committee members. Finally, directors/committee members should separate their own personal interests in the block from their role in office, and decisions should be taken, where possible, with an "objective" frame of mind.

Where particular investigations need to be carried out, it is useful for the chairman to divide/delegate the work to a "sub-committee" or "working-party". The working-party may need to meet outside the committee meetings and should report to the committee in writing by the due date.

Remuneration

Neither directors nor committee members are entitled to any remuneration for their services. In exceptional circumstances, expenses may be approved, but these should be agreed in advance with the board/committee.

A website for your block

It is a good idea, to improve communication within the block, to consider setting up a website for all lessees to access. Sometimes the cost or expertise for doing so can appear prohibitive, but some of the organisations listed in the Appendix to this book can offer helpful advice in this area.

Summary

- Every company, including an RMC, must hold an AGM every year.

- Where business of the company needs to be resolved in between AGMs, an EGM should be called.

- More informal meetings of the board of directors/residents' association committee should be held on a regular basis throughout the year.

- Proper minutes of meetings should be recorded in writing.

14 COMPANY ACCOUNTS

All buildings, however large or small, must account for the service-charge monies taken on behalf of the lessees for the proper management of their building. In addition, if your building has a resident management company or a residents' association that collects a membership subsidy, further accounting information may be required. It is important that all lessees and others dealing with the building are confident in the financial probity of the building. The accounting rules and regulations for blocks of flats are a specialised area, the detail of which is beyond the scope of this book. This chapter intends to briefly outline the different types of accounts a lessee should expect to find in respect of the building, along with the appropriate audit and tax treatments for those funds.

Types of account

As a matter of law, company directors have a duty to keep proper books and accounting records. This can be quite complex for anything but the smallest building of flats. It is always best to seek professional advice, especially because it is a criminal offence for a company not to keep proper accounting records. As a leaseholder, you should expect to see the following types of account about your building:

- service-charge account (including information regarding the reserve fund); and

- resident management company (RMC) accounts; or

- residents' association accounts (if there is no RMC and the resident association has an income).

Although it is not uncommon to find the service-charge account and the resident management company's corporate accounts intertwined, they should be accounted for separately because there is an important legal difference between them. A service-charge is defined by Section 18 of the Landlord and Tenant Act 1985 and is recoverable by law under the lease. Further explanation about service-charges can be found in Chapter 5. Company accounts are currently governed by the Companies Act 1985, but from 6 April 2008 the Companies Act 2006 will be enforceable. The accounting treatment of service-charges under the Landlord and Tenant Acts and company accounts under company law means that the service-charge account and RMC corporate accounts should be accounted for separately.

In the accounts of the RMC a leaseholder should expect to see accounting treatment for the following key items:

- annual expenditure (such as Companies House filing fee and audit fees);

- income (for example, from ground rent or other sources such as a notional rent on a resident caretaker's flat, mobile masts on the roof, various sublet storage areas/garage); and

- the notional value of the RMC's freehold asset (possibly incorporating the costs of acquiring the freehold);

Where an RMC has no income and the lessees have all been granted 999-year leases (thereby making the freehold valueless for the purposes of the balance sheet), the company may choose to file dormant accounts. This can be done using a standard form from Companies House.

It is important to clarify that service-charge funds are not part of the company's income; nor is service-charge expenditure part of the company's expenditure. Again, this stems from the fact that service-charges are recoverable under the lease and separate and distinct from company income. Indeed, service-charge funds belong to the lessees and not to the company. By contrast, ground-rent income does belong to the company. Although in many cases the lessees will also be shareholders in the company, there is, nevertheless, a significant legal distinction between the two. Service-charge monies are held in trust by the company on behalf of the lessees (who are beneficiaries of those funds). Therefore, it is misleading and confusing to find "shareholders funds" and "Service-charge funds" in the same set of accounts. A new shareholder may understand that the amount of money shown is money in the company's ownership, when this is not the case.

At the date of writing, company accounts have to be filed at Companies House within ten months of the company's financial year end. However, under proposed changes to company law, this timescale may be reduced to a filing date of six months from the company's financial year end. The accounts must contain a directors' report, which discloses the amount of shares held by each director. The accounts of the company should be distributed to all shareholders (who will invariably be the lessees of the building), considered and approved by the them at the AGM (discussed in Chapter 13). There are financial penalties if the company's accounts are not filed by the due date. If late accounts are filed on a continual basis, the company may be struck off the Register of Companies.

By comparison, there are no filing requirements for the service-charge accounts and likewise no financial penalties either. The service-charge accounts simply need to be distributed to all service-charge-paying lessees.

The audit

An audit provides an independent check and thereby an additional layer of comfort with regard to the financial statements of a company. Small companies with a turnover under £5.6 million and assets of less than £2.8 million are exempt from the requirements for an audit, although shareholders can demand one if they are concerned about the financial affairs of the company. An audit will incur additional costs for the company – ultimately these would have to be met by the shareholder-lessees. Fortunately, most RMCs will be exempt from an audit, and the accounts can be certified by the accountant or directors themselves in compliance with the requirements of the Companies Acts.

By contrast, under the Landlord and Tenant Act 1985, the service-charge accounts must be audited where the building has more than four flats. In smaller buildings, an audit need only be performed if requested by a lessee or required under the lease. Most buildings prefer to have the service-charge accounts independently verified and so always decide to have an audit.

Where the company has appointed auditors and wishes to remove them, there are specific procedures to be followed (as opposed to the reappointment of accountants, which have less onerous formalities). The auditors should be given the opportunity to present their case at the AGM as to why they consider they should not be removed.

Tax

The RMC is liable to corporation tax just like any other company. Of course, if the company is dormant, its liability will be nil. Under the Landlord and Tenant Act 1987, the service-charge fund is liable to tax at the rate applicable to trusts. Complications inevitably arise where service-charge funds are accounted for in the accounts of the RMC, instead of separately. It is advisable to seek guidance from your accountant or local HM Revenue and Customs office.

Summary

- Separate RMC accounts from service-charge accounts.

- Most RMCs will benefit from the small company audit exemption requirement.

- Make sure the company accounts are filed at Companies House on time. Queries on company accounts should not delay filing requirements. Queries can be answered later, and adjustments under particular headings can be made subsequently in the following year.

- Be aware of the difference between a "reporting accountant" and an "auditor". Not all qualified accountants register as auditors (and pay subscriptions accordingly). Carrying out an audit is a different discipline to reporting or certifying.

- As an RMC director, make sure you understand the company accounts. Possibly have a meeting with the company auditor/accountant to talk through those before presenting them at the AGM. This will be more cost effective than requiring the company auditor/accountant to attend the AGM.

- Company accounts are subject to corporation tax at the prevailing rate.

- Service-charge accounts are subject to trust tax at the prevailing rate.

15 PROFESSIONAL ASSISTANCE

There are many responsibilities in being a leaseholder, and because of the amount of legislation concerning flats, it is always prudent to obtain the best-quality advice available. Trying to be a generalist or do everything yourself may at times be foolish and at others prove to be a false economy. Some blocks are fortunate in that there are people with professional skills readily available, because they either live in or own a flat in the block. Therefore, from time to time, professional assistance will inevitably be required. This chapter seeks to highlight the types of professional skills you may need to use in the course of being a leaseholder.

Reliable contractors and tradesmen

For the most part, the managing agent of the block (if it has one) will be able to suggest contractors and tradesmen suitable for particular tasks – for example, gardening, cleaning, plumbing, pest control, general building works. However, lessees can and should nominate their own suggestions for suitable contractors/tradesmen to tender for the job. Ultimately, the best person to choose is the one who can fulfil the role efficiently and cost-effectively. Therefore, it is important to understand the particular task and match the appropriate skill-set from a selection of competent contractors nominated for that job. Sometimes, suggested contractors or tradesmen may be an "interested party", in that they are friends, relatives or business associates of the managing agent or lessees in the block. It is advisable to ascertain if any of these relationship exists or to insist on an arm's-length relationship with the preferred contractor/ tradesmen. In the event that things go wrong, personal relationships can sometimes interfere with and delay swift resolution to problems.

There may be circumstances where several lessees all nominate persons for a particular job. The following suggestions may help decide who is best to use. It is important to select a professional with the appropriate qualifications in the field of expertise you are looking for. Make sure the person or organisation is a member of the appropriate trade body (which may also be a good source for locating an appropriate contractor), as well as any employees (s)he may use on site. It is advisable to seek references about their work, and in doing so it is always best to talk to referees directly or visit sites where they have undertaken previous work rather than rely on written statements or photographs presented to you. Ideally, you should look for contractors/tradesmen who are familiar with working with blocks of flats who have had similar problems. For additional reassurance, you may want to confirm details about their identity – for example, by checking their company's registration at Companies House and discovering who the directors or partners in the business are. Finally, confirm that the contractor/tradesman has the appropriate amount of employer's and public-liability insurance cover.

Once you have selected the person or organisation for the task in hand, you should agree terms in writing. Some contractors/tradesmen will have standard terms and conditions and formal contracts to be signed. In other cases, a written letter of instruction will suffice, and it is advisable for this to be signed in duplicate with each party retaining a copy. Be wary about agreeing anything orally, because disputes can later arise about what was said. If verbal instructions are given, then they should be confirmed in writing soon afterwards as a contemporaneous record of what was said.

Managing agent

Most blocks benefit from the services of a good managing agent. Even if your block has recently enfranchised and purchased the freehold so that you can determine who manages your block, it is all but the smallest blocks who have the necessary time, skills, experience or knowledge to undertake the management themselves. A good managing agent will add value to your block over the long term. The common parts of the building will be well maintained, there will be a healthy reserve fund and service-charges will be competitive.

As many leaseholders will testify, there can be significant variance in quality between managing agents. If you are having an issue with your current managing agent, as a first step, see if a different property manager within the same company can manage your block better. Some blocks see enfranchisement as the answer, and depending on the circumstances, this may be the best solution. An alternative, which may be quicker and less expensive, is for your block to exercise its right-to-manage. Both enfranchisement and right-to-manage are dealt with in more detail elsewhere in this book.

Solicitor

There may be frequent occasions when you will need legal advice as a leaseholder, such as breach of lease covenant, variation of lease, service-charge disputes, nuisance claims, enfranchisement or leasehold valuation tribunal (LVT) representation. It is important when instructing solicitors to ensure that they are specialists in their field. A family lawyer, for example, may not necessarily be the best solicitor to deal with a protracted service-charge or breach-of-covenant dispute. There are many ways to find the best solicitor for a particular legal problem, and there are some useful starting points in the Appendix to this book. The Law Society (from whom all solicitors must hold a current practising certificate), for example, can help provide you with a list of solicitors who specialise in a particular area.

Accountant and auditor

If your block has a resident management company (RMC), you will almost certainly need the services of a good accountant to help prepare your accounts and possibly audit the company. Choosing the best accountant for the role is similar to choosing the right solicitor. Make sure that the accountant has experience in the preparation of RMC accounts. Sometimes your managing agent can help suggest names of accountants who specialise in this area.

Surveyor

Although some surveyors also have a residential property management practice, you will certainly need the advice of a surveyor for major works. Make sure the surveyor you choose is a member of the Royal Institute of Chartered Surveyors, whose members are qualified and experienced professionals.

Engineer

There are three types of engineer you may need to seek advice from about your block:

– **structural engineer** – for cracking giving rise to concern, structural movement or in relation to the building structure. Use a member of the Institute of Structural Engineers.

- **civil engineer –** relating to subsidence in pathways, roadways and
  ground external to the structure of the building. Use a member of the
  Institute of Civil Engineers.

- **Lift engineer –** do not assume that a property manager or a lift
  maintenance person can supervise the replacement or complete
  refurbishment of a lift.

Insurance broker

As explained previously in this book, insurance is not only a legal
requirement but also an important part of the efficient running of a block.
There are essentially three types of insurance cover a block/leaseholder
will need: buildings insurance, directors' and officers' insurance, and
contents insurance (optional). There are specialist insurers for some
or all of these areas, and one of the best ways to make sure you obtain
the most competitive quote is to use an insurance broker. The British
Insurance Brokers Association can also provide guidance in this area.

Company secretarial services

At present, RMCs must have a company secretary (whose roles and duties
have been explained previously in this book). Although the requirement
for a company secretary may not be compulsory under proposed changes
to company law that may soon become law, the particular nature of an
RMC will mean, at the very least, someone will need to be responsible
for issuing new share certificates when a flat is sold and concurrently
updating the share register. Many RMCs choose to offload this burden
to a company specialising in company secretarial services or a firm of
solicitors or accountants who do this type of work.

Summary

- Always select the most appropriate professional for the job after obtaining at least two quotes and carrying out appropriate verification of the person or organisation you will be dealing with.

- Agree contracts or instructions in writing.

16 A NOTE ON DISPUTE RESOLUTION

Disputes involving flats are, unfortunately, all too common. There are so many competing interests involved that inevitably fractures will emerge, especially when set against such a complex legal backdrop (the detail of which is beyond the scope of this book). In fact, by the early 1990s the situation had reached such a desperate stage that the Leasehold Advisory Service (LEASE) was set up with a specific mandate to become a government-funded advisory service to members of the public with disputes involving their flat. Now, LEASE regularly advises at least 30,000 people every year. If you are a leaseholder with a dispute stemming from your block, this chapter explains some routes to resolving those issues that arise from time to time.

© www.newsontheblock.com

Solving problems before they arise

The most common causes of neighbourly disputes are noise nuisance (probably the most common and most emotive), building works being carried out outside permitted hours, odour, smoking in the common areas, leaking rubbish sacks being left outside flat doors and indiscriminate rubbish disposal. Some of these issues have already been covered in more detail in Chapter 7.

The first step in trying to prevent a potential problem escalating into a major dispute is to approach the neighbour in question in an amicable, friendly, conciliatory and factual manner. It is understood that some people do not wish to address issues on a face-to-face basis but would prefer to do this in writing. If written communication is preferred, it should be structured in a similarly friendly and factual manner, omitting emotional utterances or threats. Always give the benefit of the doubt – the person causing the problem may not be aware of their responsibilities, the terms of the lease, or the vagaries of noise travelling through the block. If it is appropriate, allow a reasonable time scale in which to obtain resolution. Check the terms of your lease for specific prohibitions - for example, no music after 11 pm and before 8 am. Always adopt a reasonable approach and diarise events so that you have specific information at your disposal. If the first communication does not work, follow up with a second one enclosing a copy of the first. Again, where possible, be specific in terms of times, dates, and the actual lease covenant being breached if that is relevant. In the case of sublet flats, always bear in mind that it is ultimately the owner of the flat who is responsible and who will be held to account for the actions of their tenants. Contractually, the flat-owner will have to rely on the subtenancy covenants under the tenancy agreement in place and these should always mirror those imposed on the leaseholder.

Sometimes, however, trying to solve a problem in this way does not reach a successful conclusion.

How to complain

Assuming that all your reasonable efforts as listed above have been unsuccessful, you may need to take the matter further. Most nuisances have to be reported to the environmental health officer. While it is courtesy and good record-keeping to report these nuisances to a resident porter/managing agent/directors of resident management company or indeed freeholder, ultimately the powers will lie with the environmental health officer. In the case of noise, odour, smoking, noisy building works outside hours and such like, it is ultimately in the power of the environmental health officer to define what constitutes a statutory nuisance and to serve an order accordingly.

As mentioned in Chapter 7, most leases have a clause which obliges the freeholder or resident management company (RMC) to enforce the covenants of the other lessees but will require an indemnity for costs (usually under the terms of the lease). The freeholder or RMC is under no obligation to take action unless the covenant enforceability clause is in the lease. If you have reached the stage of making a formal complaint, this should always be in writing. A verbal report is useless if the cause of the particular problem is, to your knowledge, a subtenant. It is appreciated that you will not always know the identity or current address of the leaseholder. In this instance, write to the managing agent and request the managing agent to pass your correspondence on to the flat-owner in question. Keep your correspondence factual, and wherever possible corroborate with witnesses. If you are considering a letter from your own solicitor, make sure that you have all the facts available and the possibility of corroboration by independent witnesses. In extreme cases, any member of the public has the right to ask the police or local authority to apply to the courts for an ASBO. They will assess, based on the evidence, whether this is appropriate.

ADR and mediation

Before a dispute escalates into civil proceedings, you should always give consideration to whether mediation or alternative dispute resolution is more appropriate, effective over the longer term, and less costly than legal action. It is also worth checking your lease to see if it contains an arbitration clause relating to your particular problem. Resolving a dispute in this way has several distinct advantages: cost, privacy and speed to resolution. A mediation is an informal process whereby the parties gather in a private setting with a mediator. The mediator is impartial and is normally a trained expert in the particular area of dispute, though is not necessarily a lawyer. There is no need to be legally represented at a mediation. If a solution to the dispute is reached, it is recorded in writing and signed by both parties. In some circumstances, the parties can agree to a binding mediation.

Although there are several commercial mediation companies that charge for their mediation service, LEASE has recently launched its own mediation scheme, and there is no cost to participate.

The leasehold valuation tribunal

The leasehold valuation tribunal (LVT) is the part of the judicial system that adjudicates on disputes involving residential leasehold property. LVTs were conceived as quasi-judicial bodies to handle disputes in an inexpensive, efficient and effective manner. Otherwise, such disputes would have to be dealt with by the court system.

Each LVT comprises a chairman and two other panel members. The chairman is normally a lawyer or a valuer, while the other two panel members are lawyers, valuers or lay persons.

Headquartered in London but with regional tribunal centres, the LVT is normally the first port of call for a leaseholder with a dispute concerning his property. Although decisions of the LVT are binding upon the litigants, there is a limited right of appeal to the Lands Tribunal.

The LVT may hear many types of application, including those in the following key areas:

Leasehold enfranchisement: When leaseholders decide to purchase the freehold of their building, the LVT may be asked to determine the terms of the purchase and the price payable.

Lease extensions: When a leaseholder wants to extend the lease on his flat, the LVT may be asked to determine the terms of the extension and the price payable.

Service-charges: Either the landlord or the leaseholder can apply to the LVT to determine the liability to pay and the reasonableness of service-charges, either before or after works or services have commenced. Leaseholders should be aware that payment of the service-charge demanded will not be considered by the LVT as evidence of an agreement or admission by them that the service-charge is payable or reasonable. In making its decision, the LVT will consider factors such as:

- whether the works or services are (or were) necessary;

- whether the original specification for the works or services are (or were) adequate;

- the landlord's procedures for estimating the costs of the works or services;

- the landlord's procedures for controlling costs;

- whether the standard of the works or services is (or was) appropriate;

– the landlord's procedures for ensuring the works or services are (or were) delivered to the agreed specification;

– the amount (if any) that the leaseholder(s) should pay as an interim charge

Insurance: Leases sometimes provide that the leaseholders must insure with the landlord's nominated or approved insurer. The LVT may be asked to determine whether the insurance available through the landlord's nominated or approved insurer is unsatisfactory, or the premiums payable for such insurance are excessive.

Right-to-manage: The right-to-manage is contained within Chapter 1, Part 2 of the Commonhold and Leasehold Reform Act 2002. The right is exercisable simply by the service of a notice. The LVT will determine disputes, costs and issues such as:

– where the landlord or other party to be served with the claim notice is not traceable;

– where the amount of the accrued uncommitted service-charges must be determined;

– granting approvals under the lease;

– permission to exercise the right-to-manage within four years of a previous application;

Lease-variation: Any party to a lease of a flat may make an application for the terms of the lease to be varied pursuant to Sections 35-40 of the Landlord and Tenant Act 1987 if it fails to make satisfactory provision for:

– the repair and maintenance of the flat/installations/services;

- the calculation of the service-charges;

- the payment of interest on service-charge arrears;

- the recovery of expenditure incurred by one party to benefit another party to the lease; or

- any other matter.

When an individual leaseholder makes an application in respect of one flat, any other party to the lease may apply to the LVT to request the variation ordered should apply to one or more other leases. Similarly, an application can be made to vary two or more leases in the building to correct the same defect in the lease. Depending on the number of leases to be varied, 75 per cent or more of the leaseholders must consent to the variation for it to be ordered. The LVT may also order compensation to be paid to any party who is likely to be disadvantaged by the variation; if the disadvantage cannot be remedied by compensation, then the lease may not be varied.

However, it is not always easy to achieve 100 per cent agreement to an amicable lease variation. The lease-variation procedure is intended by the legislation to cater for the better, more equitable management of the block as a whole. However, it is not a mechanism designed to benefit the individual at the expense of others.

With enfranchisement becoming popular, many lessees have granted themselves new 999-year leases once in control of the freehold. During the course of enfranchisement, many arguments are emerging based on the desire of some to change the new long leases. Often, desired improvements to the lease include mandatory consent to sublet and a more expert method of calculating the service-charge. Bear in mind that material changes to the new leases could potentially involve significant litigation and legal work and may not always be successful it is not that simple to take away someone's rights that are embodied in their contract - that is, the lease. Nevertheless, it is prudent to be mindful of this developing area.

Consultation requirements: A landlord can apply to the LVT for dispensation from the consultation requirements contained in Section 20, Landlord and Tenant Act 1985. The law requires a landlord to consult with all service-charge payers in writing before carrying out works costing any one leaseholder more than £250, or before entering into a contract lasting more than 12 months that will cost an individual leaseholder more than £100 per accounting period.

Forfeiture: Forfeiture has been discussed previously in this book. The procedure is triggered by a breach of the lease and commences with the service of a notice on the leaseholder by the landlord under Section 146 of the Law of Property Act 1925. However, under Sections 168-170 of the Commonhold and Leasehold Reform Act 2002 the LVT must determine whether a breach of the lease has taken place and give the leaseholder 14 days to remedy the breach.

Administration charges: On application pursuant to Section 158 and Schedule 11 of the Commonhold and Leasehold Reform Act 2002, the LVT can consider the reasonableness of the charge, the liability of the leaseholder to pay and for a variation of a charge fixed by the lease.

Estate charges under estate management schemes: An estate management scheme under Section 159 of the Commonhold and Leasehold Reform Act 2002 requires those living within the scheme area (including freeholders) to contribute financially towards the preservation and maintenance of the area. Similar to administration charge applications, the LVT can be asked to determine the reasonableness of the charge, the liability of those within the scheme to pay and for a variation of a charge fixed by the scheme.

The appointment of a manager: Leaseholders may ask the LVT to appoint a manager for the building in "just and convenient" circumstances pursuant to Section 24 Landlord and Tenant Act 1987 where:

- they are not satisfied with the management of their building; and

- the right-to-manage is unavailable; and

- no other remedy is available.

The right to appoint a manager is not available where the landlord is a local authority, the Commission for New Towns, an urban development corporation, the Housing Corporation, a registered housing association, a fully mutual housing association or a charitable housing trust. In addition, it is not available where the landlord is resident on the premises and the building is a converted property and less than 50 per cent of the flats are let on long leases.

Limitation of landlord's legal costs: Often, a lease will provide that any legal costs incurred by a landlord (such as going to court or an LVT) can be reclaimed from all the leaseholders via the service-charges they pay. This is irrespective of whether the landlord or the leaseholder commenced the legal proceedings. Therefore, on application by a leaseholder pursuant to Section 20(c) of the Landlord and Tenant Act 1985, the LVT may determine whether it is "just and reasonable" for all or part of the landlord's legal costs to be recharged to the service-charge.

In order to make an application to the LVT, it is important that the correct form is completed. Forms are available from your local LVT or can be downloaded from the LVT website (www.rpts.gov.uk). The party making the application is known as the "applicant". Most applications require the payment of the fee, which can be as much as £500, although there are circumstances where the fee is reduced, waived or reimbursed. Full details of the fees are set out in the Leasehold valuation tribunal (Fees) Regulations 2003 or by consulting with your local LVT office.

Depending on the type of application, notice of the application may need to be given to the other parties concerned by way of formal service. The LVT will require evidence of service to be produced before allowing the application to proceed. At this stage, the LVT will process the application and send a copy to the party defending the application, known as the "respondent". However, if the LVT considers the application to be frivolous, vexatious or an abuse of process, then the application will be dismissed. This can occur either with the LVT acting upon its own motion or in response to a request by the respondent to the application. However, the applicant will be given an opportunity to resist the dismissal of the application.

Before the hearing stage of the proceedings, the LVT may hold one or more interim hearings (called pre-trial reviews) and/or issue directions to the parties with regard to the exchange of evidence and the general conduct of the case. It is important to follow the directions given by the LVT carefully. Sometimes several leaseholders bring separate applications that are based on the same substantial issue (such as, liability to pay service-charges). In these circumstances, the LVT will choose one case to be heard as representative of all the cases.

No oral hearing will take place until all the application fees have been paid. In simple cases, there will be no oral hearing, but the LVT will make a determination upon the submission of written evidence by each party. In all other cases, an oral hearing will be held to determine the outcome of the application. Usually at least 21 days' notice will be given of the hearing. The hearing itself is relatively informal and open to the public. Each party will be given an opportunity to present their case, including the presentation of evidence and witnesses (although no oath is sworn). The LVT panel may ask questions. Some parties, particularly landlords, use solicitors and barristers to present their case. Although there is no requirement for professional legal representation, in complex cases it can be helpful.

Following the hearing, the LVT will make a decision that it will deliver in writing as soon as possible after the hearing. Unless an appeal against the decision is made within four weeks, the decision is final and may be enforced in the same way as a County Court order.

There is no automatic right to appeal and any appeal, against a decision requires the permission of the LVT. To obtain permission, an application must be made to the LVT within 21 days of the decision. If the LVT refuses permission, an application must be made to the Lands Tribunal for permission to appeal. However, if the Lands Tribunal refuses permission then that is the end of the matter and the decision the LVT made is considered final. Summaries and analysis of LVT decisions are available on subscription from The LVT Bulletin (www.lvtbulletin.com).

Finally, it is prudent to mention costs, since this will be a persistent source of apprehension for leaseholders when considering an application to the LVT. The general rule is that each party is liable for their own legal costs connected with the application. The landlord, however, will often try to recover its legal costs through the service-charge, and the leaseholder may need to make a further application to limit the amount recoverable (as explained above). In addition, the LVT itself may determine that a party to the proceedings should pay the costs of another party in relation to circumstances:

– where the application has been dismissed by the LVT for being frivolous, vexatious or an abuse of process; or

– where a person has acted "frivolously, vexatiously, abusively, disruptively or otherwise unreasonably in connection with the proceedings".

The maximum award that can be made in these limited circumstances is £500. Therefore, because the costs involved in bringing an application to the LVT can be substantial, it is worth obtaining advice in advance either from a solicitor or the Leasehold Advisory Service (whose details can be found in the Appendix to this book).

The County Court

The County Court is an ordinary civil court that acts as a court of first instance for many types of civil disputes, including those relating to property. Complicated civil disputes are heard by the High Court.

In respect of leasehold property, the County Court will most commonly deal with disputes involving breach of contract, debt arrears (such as non-payment of rent), possession, squatting or those cases falling outside the jurisdiction of the LVT.

Cases are heard by a district or circuit judge, whose decision is binding upon the litigants. Appeals are made to the High Court and/or the Court of Appeal.

The Lands Tribunal

The Lands Tribunal is the part of the judicial system that adjudicates on disputes involving land.

Cases are normally heard by a single member, who is a lawyer, but in complicated cases may be assisted by a member-valuer.

The Lands Tribunal has limited jurisdiction to hear disputes relating to land (not just leasehold property) as well as appeal cases from the LVT.

Appeals from the Lands Tribunal must be made to the Court of Appeal.

The power to award costs in the Lands Tribunal is similar to that in the LVT.

Summary

- Try to settle disputes before they escalate. Talk to your neighbours. Be reasonable. Stick to the facts.

- Before becoming involved in legal proceedings, consider mediation. LEASE offers a free mediation service to leaseholders.

- As a last resort, take your dispute to court for resolution. Depending on the type of dispute legal, proceedings will need to be issued initially in either the County Court or leasehold valuation tribunal.

- Consider your exposure to costs before becoming embroiled in expensive litigation. If appropriate, seek guidance from a solicitor or the Leasehold Advisory Service – particularly before commencing a case in the County Court or making an application to the Lands Tribunal.

APPENDICES

APPENDIX 01:
Key Acts and Regulations Affecting Leaseholders

Unfortunately, the body of law affecting leaseholders is not contained within any single Act of Parliament. Instead, there is a complex matrix of Acts and Regulations by which leaseholders must comply. Following is a list of the most important Acts and Regulations affecting leaseholders. I am grateful to Robert Levene of the Federation of Private Residents' Associations for inspiring the creation of this list, which I have since developed. The following templates are for information purposes only and are not intended to be used as precedents. No responsibility for loss occassioned by any person acting or not acting as a result of this material can be accepted by the author or

KEY ACTS

- Law of Property Act 1925

- Landlord and Tenant Act 1954

- The Leasehold Reform Act 1967

- The Landlord and Tenant Act 1985

- The Landlord and Tenant Act 1987

- The Local Government and Housing Act 1989 (schedule 10)

- The Leasehold Reform, Housing and Urban Development Act 1993

- The Housing Act 1996

- The Commonhold and Leasehold Reform Act 2002

- Housing Act 2005

OTHER ACTS AND REGULATIONS

- Consumer Protection Act 1987

- Trustee Act 2000

- Financial Services & Markets Act 2000 (Consequential Amendments)

- Building Societies Act 1986

- Health & Safety at Work Act 1974

- Estate Agency Act 1979

- Property Misdescriptions Act 1991

- Race Relations Act 1976 as amended by Race Relations (Amendment) Act 2000

- Disability Discrimination Act 1995

- Disability Discrimination Act 2005

- Proceeds of Crime Act 2002

- Human Rights Act 1998

- Sex Discrimination Act 1975

- Data Protection Act 1998

- Banking Act 1987

- Cheques Act 1992

- Defective Premises Act 1972

- Employment Act 2002

- Employer's Liability (Compulsory Insurance) Act 196

- Environment Protection Act 1990

- Electricity at Work Act 1989

- Factories Act 1961

- Finance Act 1995

- Income & Corporation Taxes Act 1988

- Protection from Eviction Act 1977

- Rent Act 1977

- Trustee Investments Act 1961

- Construction Payment Act 1999

- The Service-charge Contributions (Authorised Investments) Order

- Commonhold and Leasehold Reform Act 2002, Commencement No 1 Order 2002

- Leasehold Reform (collective enfranchisement) (counter notices) (England) Regulations 2002

- Leasehold Reform (notices) (amendment) No 2 (England)Regulations 2002

- Commencement Order No 2 (England) 2003 No 1986

- Leasehold Reform (enfranchisement and extension) (England) Regulations 2003

- Leasehold Reform (collective enfranchisement and lease renewal) (amendment) (England) 2003

- The Service-charges (Consultation Requirements) (England) Regulations 2003

- The Right-to-manage (prescribed particulars and forms) (England) Regulations 2003

- The Right-to-manage (memorandum and articles of association) (England) Regulations 2003

- LVT's (fees) (England) Regulations 2003

- LVT's (procedure) (England) Regulations 2003

- Commonhold and Leasehold Reform Act 2002 (commencement no 3) Order 2003

- The Service-charges (consultation requirements) (amendment)(England) Regulation 2004

- The Commonhold Regulations 2004

- The Commonhold (land registration) Rules 2004

- Commonhold and Leasehold Reform Act Commencement Order Number 4 2004

- Commonhold and Leasehold Reform Act (commencement No 5 and saving and transitional provision) Order 2004

- The Rights of Re-entry and Forfeiture (prescribed sum and period) (England) Regulations 2004

- The Landlord and Tenant (notice of rent) (England) Regulations 2004

- The Leasehold Houses (notice of insurance cover) (England) Regulations 2004

- The Leasehold valuation tribunals (procedure) (amendment) (England) Regulations 2004

- The Electricity at Work Regulations 1989

- The Gas Safety (Installation & Use) Regulations 1998

- The Control of Substance Hazardous to Health Regulations 2002

- Control of Asbestos at Work Regulations 2002

- Control of Asbestos at Work Regulations 1987 (as amended)

- The Private Water Supplies Regulations 1991

- Management of Health & Safety Work Regulations 1999

- Furniture & Furnishing (Fire) (Safety) Regulations 1998

- The Income Tax (Sub-Contractors in the Construction Industry) Regulations 1998

- Employer's Liability (Compulsory Insurance) General Regulations 1998

- Transfer of Undertakings Protection of Employment Regulations 1981

- Transfer of Undertakings Protection of Employment Regulations 2006

- Personal Protective Equipment at Work Regulations 1992

- Lifting Operations and Lifting Equipment Regulations 1998

- The Unfair Terms in Consumer Contracts Regulations 1999

- Health & Safety (Safety Signs & Signals) Regulations 1996

- Fire Protection (Workplace) Regulations 1997

- Electrical Equipment (Safety) Regulations 1994

- Construction (Design & Management) Regulations 1994

- Construction (Health Safety and Welfare) Regulations 1996

- Provision and Use of Work Equipment Regulations 1992

- Pressure Systems & Transportable Gas Containers Regulations 1989

- Money Laundering Regulations 2003

- Home Information Pack Regulations 2006

- Companies Act 2006

- Smoke Free Regulations 2006 and 2007

APPENDIX 02:
Welcome Pack and House Rules

Following is a suggested template for the preparation of a welcome pack and house rules for your block. The information contained in the following template is intended for guidance purposes only and should not be relied upon as accurate or binding.

Welcome Pack and House Rules
For Leaseholders and Tenants

Acacia Mansions (Management) Ltd
Acacia Road
Acacia AC1 1CC

Date

1. Introduction and Welcome

We are delighted to welcome you as our neighbour to Acacia Mansions, whether as a fellow leaseholder or as a tenant. In this welcome pack we hope to introduce you to the block and answer some of the most common questions you may have. You may find it useful to keep this guide as a reference tool, and you can also find a copy on our website. If you have any questions, please get in touch.

We hope that you will enjoy a happy time living here!

John Jones

Chairman
Acacia Mansions (Management) Ltd
johnjones@acaciamansionsltd.com
Tel: 020 9987 7890

2. About our Block

Acacia Mansions is owned and managed by Acacia Mansions (Management) Ltd. All leaseholders as owners of flats in Acacia Mansions have a share in the company. We employ a managing agent to help us run the block day to day collect our service-charges and ground rent. The details of the managing agent can be found below.

We have appointed a board of directors to control the running of the block on a day to day basis. All members of the board own flats in the block and carry out their duties voluntarily in the interests of everyone here. The board meets on a monthly basis and does not get paid for voluntary work. If you would like to contact the board or volunteer to become a director, please contact John Jones, the chairman of the board using the details found at the beginning of this pack.

3. About our Residents' Association

We are proud to say that we have a thriving residents' association in the block. Although the residents' association is independent of the company, some of the directors are also members of the residents' association. The residents' association concentrates on making the community life in the block as pleasant as possible. For example, we liaise with the local neighbourhood watch and the police regarding security in the block.

We would be delighted if you would like to become a member of our residents' association. Membership is free – please contact the head porter for more details.

4. Our Managing Agent

We are proud to have as our managing agents Build and Block Management Ltd. Build and Block has been managing our block for many years and have always been extremely helpful in sorting out any issues we may have. If you need to contact Build and Block, our property manager is Mr Bob Smith and his details are:

Build and Block Management Ltd
Build and Block House
Build and Block Road
Tel: 01200 123 456
Fax: 01200 321 654
Web: www.buildandblockltd.com
Email: bobsmith@buildandblockltd.com

5. Our Block's Website

We have recently launched a new website for the block, in association with News on the Block – the magazine all about flats. The website provides a value added communication tool for the block, and we hope you find it a useful source of information and a forum to discussion. There is no cost to use the website.

To use the website, you will first need to become a registered user. This only takes a few minutes, and you can do so by visiting www.newsontheblock.com and following the on-screen instructions.

If you have any suggestions about ways in which we can improve the website, please let the website administrator know.

6. Register of Owners, Tenants and Emergency Contacts

The Head Porter maintains a register of owners, tenants and emergency contacts. Please make sure that he has the current details in respect of your flat.

7. Familiarising Yourself with the Block

a. House staff

With such a large block, we require several members of in-house staff to look after the building. Our head porter, Mr James Smythson, has been with us for 20 years. He is always friendly and helpful. He is in charge of the security, daily mainteance, cleaning and gardening.

Mr Smythson has a team of two part-time uniformed caretakers to help him, but in the first instance you should direct any questions to him. We are fortunate that Mr Smythson lives in the block. He lives in Flat 1 and his telephone number is: 020 9345 6789. However, please be aware that he is only on duty Monday-Friday 8.00am-4.30pm. Outside these hours, Mr Smythson is on call for emergencies only. If, for some reason, you cannot contact him, please contact the managing agents instead.

Aside from Mr Smythson and his team, we also have a team of cleaners and gardeners who you will regularly see around the block.

b. Gardens

The communal gardens in the block are for the enjoyment of all residents. However, please keep noise to a minimum and refrain from playing ball games.

c. Rubbish

There are communal bins located on every floor. Please bag or wrap your domestic rubbish securely and place in the bins provided. Rubbish is removed and collected from the building twice a week.

For the disposal of larger items such as white goods, flat-owners must arrange a collection from the local authority. Please contact the head porter or see our website for further details.

d. Recycling

This block also encourages recycling, and there is a specially marked recycling bin on every floor. There is no need to separate your recylcable material – just place it in the bin provided.

e. Parking

There is limited parking in the block car park at the rear of the building. Parking is available by permit to flat-owners on a first come, first served basis. Permits are issued by the head porter against a list of owners. We regret that there is no parking available for tenants, but residents' and meter parking is available in the roads adjacent to the block. Please note that if a car is parked in the block without a permit, it is liable to be clamped or removed by our parking control service.

f. CCTV

For the security and safety of all residents, visitors, staff and contractors, this block operates a CCTV system.

g. Television reception

There are analogue television aerial connections in all flats. In addition, you can obtain cable television. Please contact the Head Porter for further details.

Under no circumstances are residents allowed to install their own television aerials or satellite dishes. This is a breach of the lease and will result in legal action.

h. The roof

There is a small area on the roof designated as a sundeck, in good weather only. This is clearly marked. All other areas of the roof are strictly out of bounds and should not be used. If a contractor needs access, please contact the head porter in advance.

i. Lifts

We have two passenger lifts in the block. Only one may be used when you are moving in/out of your flat. Please respect the weight requirements clearly specified on the lift and refrain from taking heavy items, furniture or soiled items in the lifts.

j. Bicycles

A bicycle rack is provided at the front of the block. As there is only limited space, you must have a permit to park your bike there. Permits cost £20 per annum and are payable in advance. Please contact the head porter, who will issue you with a key.

If you are not using the bicycle rack provided, please do not store bicycles in the communal areas or chain them to any other external area of the block. Also, do not wheel bicycles through the communal areas.

k. Notice board

The notice board is situated in the communal entrance foyer. Official notices are placed here. There is also space for you to place notices of your own. Please be courteous to other users of the notice board. You may also like to visit the website for our block, which also has a notice board.

8. Common questions about the lease

a. Subletting

Although subletting is permitted under the lease, you will need to acquire the appropriate permission via the managing agent. If you do not, you will be in breach of the lease and subject to legal action. All subtenants must be vetted in advance, and you must ensure that they have a copy of these House Rules.

b. Other provisions in the lease

While we do not intend to repeat the contents of your lease here, please be aware of the following key provisions:

i. Your windows must be kept clean and must have blinds or curtains. You must not hang washing outside your window.

ii. You must not paint your front door a different colour to all the other flats in the building.

iii. You may not use your flat as a place of work – it is for residential use only.

c. Insurance

The building is insured under a policy arranged by the company. All flat-owners contributed to the insurance premium in their service-charges. If you need to make a claim, please refer to the insurance-claim procedure, which can be obtained by contacting the managing agent or looking on the website for our block.

In addition, you may consider organising your own contents insurance for your flat. Such items will not be covered by the buildings insurance.

d. Service-charges

All flat-owners pay a quarterly sum in advance towards the maintenance of the building. You will be sent an invoice from the managing agent informing you how much you need to pay. We ask that flat-owners pay their service-charges promptly on demand so that maintenance cannot be interrupted. Late payment may be met with legal action and, under the lease, you will be liable for all associated legal costs. We use the service-charge monies for maintenance expenditure, which includes: heating, electricity, water, cleaning, professional fees and staff salaries.

9. What to Do in Event of Fire?

If you find a fire, call the emergency services immediately by dialing 999 on your telephone. Also, contact a member of the House Staff without delay.

There are fire extinguishers in every hallway and at the front entrance. If you are not trained to use them, you should concentrate on escaping from the building as quickly as possible. Do not wait or try to deal with the fire yourself.

Do not use the lifts when trying to exit the building. Use the stairs. If you see any communal doors open, please close them – they also act as fire doors.

For the safety of all of us, we carry out a fire-risk assessment regularly on the building.

10. Staying Safe: Security in the Buiding

As you can appreciate, living in a prime central urban location as we do carries with it a security risk. We ask all residents to help maintain the security within the block by being vigilant at all times. There are some simple things you can do to help ensure the security of the building is not compromised:

i. Complete a keyholder emergency contact form
ii. Do not leave communal access doors open or unlocked.
iii. Do not let anyone into the block who you do not know, even if they say they live in the block or are visiting someone who does.
iv. Report any suspicious people loitering in or around the block to the head porter immediately.

11. Complaints and Queries

If you have any complaints or queries about the block, in the first instance contact the head porter or property manager.

12. Frequently Asked Questions?

a. Contractors

Only approved contractors who are members of their appropriate trade body (for example, CORGI) may carry out work in the building. That includes your individual flat. Before work commences, please consult the head porter who will explain the rules and requirements of contractors working in the block. Similarly, please tell your contractors to report to the head porter on first arrival. We want to make Acacia Mansions a safe place to work, and the head porter will need to go through some health and safety procedures with your contractors.

Some work for which contractors attend the block can be noisy or disruptive to your neighbours. We ask you to exercise your utmost consideration in this respect. Ultimately, you are responsible for the conduct of your contractors while on the premises, including any repair costs. If your contractors do not comply with our rules for working in the block, they will be asked to leave.

If you would like to review a list of contractors who are available for work in the block, please contact the head porter who maintains a list.

b. Building work

If you need to do work to your flat, either because you intend to alter it or make repairs to it, please contact the managing agent in advance of commencing work. You may need to obtain a licence first. If you do not do so, you may in breach of your lease and liable to legal proceedings.

c. Working hours

Working hours in the block are Monday-Friday 8am-5pm. However, noisy work can only be carried out weekdays between 9.30am and 4pm. No contractors are permitted to work on the premises during public holidays.

d. Removals

We understand that moving in and out of the block can be a stressful experience. We try to work with you to minimise any disruption. Removals can be made Monday–Saturday 8am-6pm. Please note that one lift will be designated a removal lift during the time of your removal, and you should speak with the head porter to arrange this in advance. Aside from that, please do not cause an obstruction to the communal hallways, stairs or the other lift. If you leave any items unattended, then this is at your own risk.

e. Cleaning

Although we employ cleaners to look after the communal areas of the building, remove rubbish and polish brass surfaces (such as door handles and kick plates), we ask that all residents help them to do their job by keeping communal areas as clean as possible. Please note that cleaners are there to look after the common parts and not the inside of your internal flat.

f. Pest control

From time to time, we have had problems with pests in our block. If you experience any problems with pests, please contact the head porter immediately. High-density living means that pests may not be an isolated occurrence and can spread quickly. We do not want a single occurrence to become an infestation.

We can all do our bit to minimise the occurrence of pests, and that includes keeping our flats as clean as possible.

g. Smoking

We operate a strict no-smoking policy in the common parts of the block. If you, your visitors or contractors must smoke, then please do so inside your flat (taking care that smoke does not escape into the corridors) or outside of the building (please make sure you are well away from ground-floor windows).

h. Deliveries

Deliveries may be made to the block providing the flat-owner is in-house to receive the delivery. The house staff cannot take deliveries on behalf of residents.

i. Noise

Due to the way this block was built, noise between flats unfortunately carries quite easily. We want our block to be a peaceful environment, and therefore we ask all residents to be considerate with regard to the amount of noise made inside their flat. Please be particularly conscious of the volume of your television, how loud you play music and do not play musical instruments or have noisy parties.

j. Pets

Apart from guide dogs, no pets are allowed in the block under any circumstances.

APPENDIX 03:
Health & Safety Competence Assessment

Leaseholders may find the following form helpful to ascertain the competence of a contractor with regard to health and safety guidelines, and ensure high standards of compliance with health and safety legislation for contractors working in the block.

You may find it useful to keep this guide as a reference tool, and you can also find a copy on our website. If you have any questions, please get in touch.l

CONTRACTOR HEALTH & SAFETY ASSESSMENT
Your Name:
Company Name:
Company Address:
Company Telephone Number:
Website:
E-mail address:
General
Please provide a copy of your Health & Safety Policy.
Are you a member of a trade or professional body? (If so, please provide details.)
Do your staff or third-party contractors hold current Certificates of Competence in Health and Safety training?
Do you have Safe Method of Work guidelines for employees? How is it communicated to them?

Please provide details of any Health & Safety Advisor or Consultant employed by you.

Please provide the details of three clients, for whom you have provided services in the last 24 months as references:

1.

2.

3.

Health and Safety Procedures

Do you have procedures for:

(a) reporting accidents, injuries, deaths and dangerous occurrences?

(b) identifying training needs and training in health and safety?

(c) performing Safety Risk Assessments?

(d) performing Safety Audits?

Health and Safety History

Have you reported or notified any accident or fatality in the last two years? (If so, please provide details.)

Have you ever been prosecuted for breach of Health and Safety legislation?

Have you ever been served with an enforcement notice by the Health and Safety Executive?

Have you ever been involved in legal proceedings concerning negligence or breach of duty of care?

APPENDIX 04:
Contact Form and Emergency Keyholder Record

BLOCK CONTACT FORM	
Please complete this form and return to: [Company Address]	
Your details:	
Your flat number:	
Your name:	
Your home telephone number:	
Your mobile telephone number:	
Your email address:	
If your flat is sublet:	
Your mailing address:	
Name of subtenant:	
Home telephone number of subtenant:	
Mobile telephone number of subtenant:	
Work telephone number of subtenant:	
Email address of subtenant:	
Emergency Keyholder details:	
Name:	
Address:	
Home telephone:	
Work telephone:	
Mobile telephone:	
Email address:	

APPENDIX 05:
Notice of Annual General Meeting

NOTICE IS HEREBY GIVEN that the Annual General Meeting of ACACIA MANSIONS (MANAGEMENT) ("the Company") will be held at the ACACIA CENTRE, 123 ACACIA GARDENS, ACACIA A12 3CC on FRIDAY, 8 FEBRUARY 2008 at 6.30 pm for the following purposes:

1. To approve the minutes of the Annual General Meeting held on 8 February 2006.
2. To receive and adopt the Accounts of the Company for the financial period ended 31 March 2007.
3. To appoint Smith, Jones and McDonald as Auditors of the Company until the conclusion of the next Annual General Meeting of the Company.
4. To authorise the directors to determine the remuneration of the auditors.
5. To consider any other business of which prior written notice has been given.

By Order of the Board of Directors

J Smith
Secretary

Dated 5 December 2007

Registered Office:
Acacia Mansions (Management) Ltd
Acacia Road
Acacia AC1 1CA

NOTES

Any member of the Company wishing to have an item included under item 5 of the Agenda should notify the Secretary of the Company (c/o Build and Block Management Ltd, Build and Block House, Build and Block Road, Acacia A45 8BB) no later than seven days prior to the above meeting.

Any member of the Company entitled to attend, speak and vote at the above mentioned meeting may appoint a proxy to attend, speak and vote on that member's behalf. A proxy need not be a member of the Company. To be valid, the instrument appointing a proxy and any authority under which it is executed (or a copy of the same certified) must be deposited at the registered office of the Company (c/o Build and Block Management Ltd, Build and Block House, Build and Block Road, Acacia A45 8BB) NOT LESS THAN 48 HOURS BEFORE THE TIME OF THE MEETING.

APPENDIX 06:
DIRECTOR'S NOMINATION FORM

The Secretary
Acacia Mansions (Management) Ltd
Acacia Road
Acacia AC1 1CC

Date _____

Dear Sir

RE:

TAKE NOTICE that the undersigned shareholders intend respectively to propose and
second _____ of Flat _____
for election as a director of Acacia Mansions (Management) Limited at the Annual
General Meeting convened for Friday 8 February 2008 or any adjournment thereof.

Yours faithfully

_____(Flat No.)

_____(Flat No.)

NOTES
Not less than 14 nor more than 35 clear days before the date appointed for the Annual General Meeting written
notice, signed by a member qualified to vote at the meeting, must be given to the Company at its Registered
Office of the intention to propose a person who is a member of the Company for appointment as a director of the
Company. Such written notice must be accompanied by the consent in writing of such a nominee on the Director's
Consent Form.

APPENDIX 07:
DIRECTOR'S CONSENT FORM

To:
The Secretary
Acacia Mansions (Management) Ltd
Acacia Road
Acacia AC1 1CC

Dear Sir

RE:

Being a shareholder in the above-mentioned company, I hereby consent to being proposed as a director at the Annual General Meeting of the Company to be held on Friday 8 February 2008 or any adjournment thereof.

Yours faithfully,

Name   Flat No.   Date

(Please note: This consent form must be returned to the Registered Office with the completed Nomination Form).

APPENDIX 08:
FORM OF PROXY

I/We, of ....,being a member of the above named company and entitled to vote hereby appoint _____

____as my proxy to attend and vote for me/us on my/our behalf or, as he or she thinks fit, abstain from voting at the Annual General Meeting of the Company to be held at the ACACIA CENTRE, 123 ACACIA GARDENS, ACACIA A12 3CC at 6.30pm and at any adjournment thereof and hereby authorise him/her to sign on my/our behalf a Consent to Short Notice of the said Meeting.

Dated: _____

Signed _____

The signing of this proxy form does not preclude you from attending and voting in person at the meeting or any adjournment thereof.

NOTES

1. The Member should insert name(s) as desired, and if no nomination is made, the Proxy, in his discretion, will vote as he thinks fit or abstain from voting.

2. A proxy need not be a member of the Company.

3. Proxy forms must be returned to the Company secretary, Acacia Mansions (Management) Ltd, c/o Build and Block Management Ltd, Build and Block House, Build and Block Road, Acacia A45 8BB, no less that 48 hours before the commencement of the meeting.

4. In the case of joint holders, the vote of the senior who tenders a vote, whether in person or by proxy, shall be accepted to the exclusion of the votes of the other registered holder or holders and for this purpose seniority shall be determined by the order in which the names stand in the Register of Members in respect of the joint holding,

5. If this Form of Proxy is given by a body corporate, it must be given under its Common Seal or under the hand of an attorney or officer duly appointed.

APPENDIX 09:
SAMPLE MINUTES

Minutes of the Annual General Meeting of Acacia Mansions (Management) Limited held at the ACACIA CENTRE, 123 ACACIA GARDENS, ACACIA A12 3CC on 8 February 2008.

Present: J Jones (Chairman) (Flat 32), P Smith (Director) (Flat 48)
A McKintosh (Flat 2)
In attendance: J. Smith (Secretary), Mr B Smith of Build and Block Management Ltd

1. The Chairman proposed:
"That the minutes of the Annual General Meeting held on 8 February 2006 be approved."

Mr Smith seconded the resolution, which was put to the meeting and declared carried.

2. The Chairman proposed:
"That the Accounts for the Company for the financial period ended 31 March 2007 be received and adopted."

Mr Smith seconded the resolution, which was put to the meeting and declared carried.

3. The Chairman proposed:
"That Messrs Smith, Jones and McDonald be and are hereby appointed as Auditors of the Company, to hold office until the conclusion of the next Annual General Meeting."

Mr McKintosh seconded the resolution, which was put to the meeting and declared carried.

4. The Chairman proposed:
"That the remuneration of Messrs Smith, Jones and McDonald, the Company Auditors, be determined by the directors."

Mr McKintosh seconded the resolution, which was put to the meeting and declared carried.

5. No other business of which prior written notice had been given was considered.

There being no further business, the meeting was closed.

John Jones
Chairman, 8 February 2008

APPENDIX 10:
USEFUL ADDRESSES

News On The Block
The Essential Resource For The
Apartment Sector
One Great Cumberland Place
Marble Arch
London W1H 7AL
Tel: 08700 600 663
Fax: 08700 600 664
E-mail: info@newsontheblock.com
Website: www.newsontheblock.com

The LVT Bulletin
Exclusive summaries and analysis of
leasehold valuation tribunal decisions
One Great Cumberland Place
Marble Arch
London W1H 7AL
Tel: 08700 600 663
Fax: 08700 600 664
E-mail: circulation@lvtbulletin.com
Website: www.lvtbulletin.com

The Housing Ombudsman Bulletin
Exclusive summaries and analysis of
leasehold valuation tribunal decisions
One Great Cumberland Place
Marble Arch
London W1H 7AL
Tel: 08700 600 663
Fax: 08700 600 664
E-mail: circulation@
housingombudsmanbulletin.com
Website:
www.housingombudsmanbulletin.com

The Housing Ombudsman Service
Norman House
105-109 Strand
London WC2R 0AA
Tel: 020 7836 3630
Lo-Call: 0845 7125 973
Minicom: 020 7240 6776

Fax: 020 7836 3900
E-mail: ombudsman@hos.org.uk
Website: www.ihos.org.uk

The Association of Residential
Managing Agents (ARMA)
178 Battersea Park Road
London SW11 4ND
Telephone: 020 7978 2607
Fax: 020 7498 6153
Email: info@arma.org.uk
Website: www.arma.org.uk

The Leasehold Advisory Service
(LEASE)
31 Worship Street, London EC2A 2DX
Telephone: 020 7374 5380
Fax: 020 7374 5373
Email: info@lease-advice.org
Website: www.lease-advice.org

The Association of Residential
Letting Agents (ARLA)
Maple House
53-55 Woodside Road
Amersham
Bucks HP6 6AA
Phone: 0845 345 5752
Fax: 0149 4431 530
E-mail: info@arla.co.uk
Website: www.arla.co.uk

The National Association of Estate
Agents (NAEA)
Arbon House
21 Jury Street
Warwick CV34 4EH
Tel: 019 2649 6800
E-mail: info@naea.co.uk
Website: www.naea.co.uk

British Insurance Brokers'
Association (BIBA)
14 Bevis Marks
London EC3A 7NT
Consumer Helpline: 0870 950 1790
Fax: 020 7626 9676
E-mail: enquiries@biba.org.uk
Website: www.biba.org.uk

The Federation of Private Residents'
Associations (FPRA)
59 Mile End Road
Colchester CO4 5BU
Tel: 0871 200 3324 (calls charged at
standard national rate)
Tel: 01206 855 888
E-mail: info@fpra.org.uk
Website: www.fpra.org.uk

The Land Registry
Website: www.landreg.gov.uk
For registrations in England –
Tel: 08709 088 063.
For registrations in Wales –
Tel: 08709 088 069.

Health and Safety Executive (HSE)
Rose Court
2 Southwark Bridge
London SE1 9HS
Tel: 0845 345 0055
Website: www.hse.gov.uk

Department for Communities and
Local Government (DCLoG)
Eland House
Bressenden Place
London SW1E 5DU
Tel: 020 7944 4400 (8.30am-5.30pm
Mon-Fri)
Fax: 020 7944 4101
E-mail: contactus@communities.gsi.
gov.uk (general enquiries)
Website: www.communities.gsi.gov.uk

The Lands Tribunal
Procession House
55 Ludgate Hill
London EC4M 7JW
Tel: 020 7029 9780
Fax: 020 7029 9781
E-mail: lands@dca.gsi.gov.uk

Residential Property Tribunal
Service (RPTS) & The Leasehold
Valuation Tribunal
10 Alfred Place
London WC1E 7LR
Tel: 020 7446 7700
Fax: 020 7637 1250
Website: www.rpts.gov.uk

The Court Service
Website: www.hmcourts-service.gov.uk

The Financial Services Authority (FSA)
Website:
www.moneymadeclear.fsa.gov.uk
Leafletline 0845 456 1555
Consumer Contact Centre: 0845 606
1234 or, +44 (0)20 7066 1000

British Pest Control Association
Ground Floor
Gleneagles House
Vernongate
Derby DE1 1UP
Tel: 0870 609 2687
Fax: 013 3229 5904
E-mail: enquiry@bpca.org.uk
Website: www.bpca.org.uk

British Parking Association
Stuart House
41-43 Perrymount Road
Haywards Heath
West Sussex RH16 3BN
Tel: 01444 447 300
Email: info@britishparking.co.uk
Fax: 01444 454 105

Mobile Operators' Association
Russell Square house
10-12 Russell Square
London WC1B 5EE
Tel: 020 7331 2015
Fax: 020 7332 047
E-mail: info@ukmoa.org

**Asbestos Testing and Consulting
Association**
237 Branston Road
Burton Upon Trent
Staffordshire DE14 3BT
Tel: 012 8353 1126
Fax: 012 8356 8228
Website: www.arcaweb.org.uk

The Safety Assessment Federation
Nutmfor example,House,
60 Gainsford Street,
Butlers Wharf,
London SE1 2NY
E-mail info@safed.co.uk
Tel: 020 7403 0987
Fax: 020 7403 0137

GLOSSARY OF TERMS

TERM	MEANING
AGM	The annual general meeting of a company
Block	A building containing individual flats and common areas shared between them.
CLARA 2002	The Commonhold and Leasehold Reform Act 2002.
Common parts	Those area of a block of flats that are common to all flat-owners.
Commonhold	A new form of tenure created by the Commonhold and Leasehold Reform Act 2002. Commonhold allows for the freehold ownership of the individual flats within a block, and shared ownership of the common parts.
D&O	Directors' and officers' (usually refers to a particular type of insurance policy)
D&O	Commonly refers to directors' and officers' insurance
DDA	Disability Discrimination Act 1995 and/or Disability Discrimination Act 2005.
EGM	An extraordinary general meeting of a company
Enfranchisement	The process by which the leaseholders of a block can purchase the freehold of the building.
Forfeiture	A legal process that enables a landlord to terminate a lease where the tenant is in breach and take back possession of his property.
Freehold	Absolute ownership of a property – the most supreme form of tenure possible.
Ground rent	A nominal amount paid by the lessee to the freeholder in compensation for the use of the land by the building in which the lessee has a flat.
Landlord	Commonly the freeholder to the property. The landlord is a party to the lease and grants the use of the property for a definite period of time to the lessee. Also, known as lessor.
Lease	The property contract between a lessee and lessor, setting out the terms of agreement between them.

Lease extension	The right of the lessee to demand the landlord to extend his lease to 99 years.
Leasehold	A form of property ownership that provides the right to use and enjoy a property for a definite period of time.
Lessee	The party to a lease who is granted the right to use and enjoy the property for a definite period of time.
Lessor	See Landlord.
Managing agent	A company instructed to manage the common parts of a block of flats for a fee.
NOTB	*News on the Block* – the magazine all about flats
Property manager	The individual person employed by a managing agent responsible for managing a block of flats.
Reserve fund	A sum of money saved up over a period of time to pay for emergency works or complying with maintenance obligations in a lease. Now, this term commonly includes the term "sinking fund" too.
Resident management company	Legal entity set up to control the management of the block.
Reversionary interest	The right to receive full ownership of a flat upon the expiration of the lease term.
Right-to-manage	The right of leaseholders within a block to take control of the management of the building into their own hands. A right-to-manage company in which each participating leaseholder is a member must be formed.
RMC	Resident management company
RTE	Right to enfranchise company.
RTM	See right-to-manage.
Service-charge	An amount payable by each lessee towards the maintenance and repair of the common parts of a block of flats.
Sinking fund	A sum of money saved up over a period of time to replace a defunct item, no longer fit for its purpose. Also see Reserve fund
Tenure	The method by which property is owned. There are three types of tenure: freehold, leasehold and commonhold.
Unit	One individual flat.

Index